First Congregational Church of Stockton

A Collection of Recipes by
150th Anniversary Edition
3409 Brookside Road
Stockton, CA 95219
FirstCongregationalStockton.org/FCCS@att.net

Printed in the USA by

MORRIS PRESS
COOKBOOKS

800-445-6621 • www.morriscookbooks.com
P.O. Box 2110 • Kearney, NE 68848

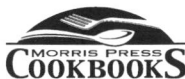

Present home of First Congregational Church Stockton 2014

In 1861 the First Congregational Church of Stockton(FCCS) opened it's doors for Sunday worshipers. Naturally there had between years of organizing, fund raising, communicating with denomination and worshiping wherever space was available. These are the steps that go into building a solid, honest church that has lasted one hundred fifty years! In addition, one can only try to picture Stockton in 1861. Luckily, California was somewhat removed from the turmoil that was tearing the country apart at the time. The Gold Rush was over, taking with it some of the unsavory characters and crime that put Stockton on the map. Apparently the farmers, business people and families wanted a church that would last (in several different locations)for one hundred fifty years. How grateful we are for their commitment, sacrifice, determination, and especially foresight as they planned as institution they wanted to last for generations.

By 1861 the Congregational Church had a distinct and highly respected position in the United Stated (U.S.) It was already known as "the Church of Firsts". Following the well known path of Protestantism after Reformation, a group known as the Pilgrims came to the U.S. seeking freedom of religion, equality of clergy and congregation, and democratic church decision making. This sect joined with the Puritans to form the first group labeled Congregational. Along the way the denomination had already taken a stand against slavery, supported civil disobedience during the Boston Tea Party, and ordained an African American pastor. These 'firsts" were followed by the development of the first school for the deaf, Abolitionist Society, support for Armistad prisoners, and the ordination of a woman to serve as pastor of her own church.

1957 saw another historic step as the United Church of Christ (UCC) was formed from the merger of Evangelical and Reformed churches, with the Congregational Christian churches. Am effort to embrace the traditions of all cultures represented within these churches was emphasized. In 1959, an historic ruling supported by UCC supported by the UCC stated that airways are public property. In 1972 the UCC ordained it's first openly gay minister in the Golden Gate Association.

As society grew, and the First Congregational Church of Stockton continued to adapt and re-interpret it's role. The large congregations of the 50's and 60's were replaced by smaller dedicated church goers who did not profess to have all the answers but were committed to sharing their hopes, questions, and deep concern for each other. As the church continued to feed the souls and hearts of the members, so also did the men and women break bread together. Our collection of recipes here represents this history, with a deep sense of joy and gratitude in this, our sesquicentennial year.

THIS AND THAT

This section could be titled "Recipes from Heaven" because each dish described here is a contribution from a devoted church member who is no longer with us. With the help of their families and friends we have been able to include signature recipes from each of our "women pioneers". More importantly, we give thanks for their gifts and talents which helped sustain FCCS through the one hundred fifty year history we are celebrating.

As the church began preparing for the sesquicentennial, a series of losses tested our resilience. The death of Ruth Cunningham, who had served as church historian, Women's Fellowship officer, and helped initiate the A'Faire was devastating. Her contributions to the broader UCC church were too numerous to count. Right before that time; Cheryl Behrns passed away, shocking the congregation who were used to seeing and hearing her singing in the church choir every Sunday as she had since girlhood in her father's Congregational church. Cheryl had organized each month's Dinner Club for years and served the church and community as an educator. Nora Imes was the most devoted Book Club member and many people didn't realize Nora had worked as a nurse at the County Hospital. This same year saw the loss of Mildred Ryckman who made tremendous contributions to Stockton's Special Education Program. We miss them all.

The Cookbook Committee began to wonder whether cooking and teaching had some special connection as we received recipes from the collections of Frances Fagler, a Nebraska native who also taught in Stockton; and Margaret Smith who taught English at Stagg High School, as did Marilyn Brown. Jeanette Anderson gave years to teaching along with the others who raised their families and volunteered in the church. Another member came to us after years of membership in Escondido's UCC. Rebecca Freeman's life even more commendable when one remembers she suffered from severe hearing disability.

Audrey Peterson left her home UCC in Boston, Massachusetts to migrate to San Francisco and eventually Stockton where she worked for a law firm and devoted herself to FCCS. Bertha Green raised her family while generously supporting the church with her unique Eastern European dishes and baked goods. Her recipes, like those of the committed environmentalist Doris Haskell, are real gifts to those interested in food and it's history. Our "Recipes from Heaven" are not only fascinating, more than anything they remind us of the pillars of the church who are still part of who we are and should never be forgotten.

Table of Contents

The original San Joaquin County courthouse where
congregation worshiped before first building.

Appetizers
& Beverages

263841-sg-1a

Helpful Hints

- Add flavor to tea by dissolving old-fashioned lemon drops or hard mint candies in it. They melt quickly and keep the tea brisk.

- Make your own spiced tea or cider. Place orange peels, whole cloves, and cinnamon sticks in a 6-inch square piece of cheesecloth. Gather the corners and tie with a string. Steep in hot cider or tea for 10 minutes; steep longer if you want a stronger flavor.

- Always chill juices or sodas before adding them to beverage recipes.

- Calorie-free club soda adds sparkle to iced fruit juices and reduces calories per portion.

- To cool your punch, float an ice ring made from the punch rather than using ice cubes. It appears more decorative, prevents diluting, and does not melt as quickly.

- Place fresh or dried mint in the bottom of a cup of hot chocolate for a cool and refreshing taste.

- When making fresh lemonade or orange juice, one lemon yields about ¼ cup juice, while one orange yields about ⅓ cup juice.

- Never boil coffee; it brings out acids and causes a bitter taste. Store ground coffee in the refrigerator or freezer to keep it fresh.

- Always use cold water for electric drip coffee makers. Use 1–2 tablespoons ground coffee for each cup of water.

- How many appetizers should you prepare? Allow 4–6 appetizers per guest if a meal quickly follows. If a late meal is planned, allow 6–8 appetizers per guest. If no meal follows, allow 8–10 pieces per guest.

- If serving appetizers buffet-style or seating is limited, consider no-mess finger foods that don't require utensils to eat.

- Think "outside the bowl." Choose brightly-colored bowls to set off dips or get creative with hollowed-out loaves of bread, bell peppers, heads of cabbage, or winter squash.

- Cheeses should be served at room temperature – approximately 70°.

- To keep appetizers hot, make sure you have enough oven space and warming plates to maintain their temperature.

- To keep appetizers cold, set bowls on top of ice or rotate bowls of dips from the fridge every hour or as needed.

APPLE DIP
Judy Craig

8 oz. cream cheese, softened
¾ c. brown sugar
1 c. caramel apple sauce

1 c. toffee baking bits
5 Fuji apple -slices**

Blend together cream cheese and brown sugar, then top with caramel apple sauce. Sprinkle toffee bits on top. Arrange sliced apples around plate for dipping. Serve at room temperature. ** Put slices of apple in bowl of lemon-lime soda to prevent browning, then drain before serving.

ARTICHOKE CHIP DIP
Susie Freas

1 c. cream cheese
1 c. mayonnaise

1 can artichoke hearts
garlic salt and pepper to taste

Mix in food processor or blender. Bake at 375° for 20-25 minutes. Serve with pita chips

BRAUNSCHWEIGER CANAPÉ
Susie Freas
Frances Evans

2 cans beef consomme
2 unflavored gelatin (Knox)
1 lb. liverwurst
8 oz. cream cheese

a bit of grated onion
4 drops Worcestershire sauce
2-3 dashes garlic salt
sliced olives

Heat consomme and dissolve gelatin in it. Oil a mold (approx. 1 qt. or two ice cube trays). After slicing the olives, arrange them on bottom of mold. Pour a thin layer of the heated consomme on olives and put into freezer for 5 min. or until hardened. Mix cheese and liverwurst together and add rest of seasonings. Beat until smooth. Pour over the hardened olive mixture. This recipe will keep in refrigerator for 3 weeks. Before serving, unmold. Recipe may be easily divided in half..

BROCCOLI-FETA SQUARES
Regina Brown

4 eggs
½ c. oil
1 10 oz. frozen broccoli,
    thawed & squeezed dry
½ c. chopped onion

½ c. feta cheese
⅓ c. Parmesan cheese, grated
1 t. dill weed
1 c. buttermilk baking mix

Heat oven to 350°. Beat eggs with oil, then add broccoli, onion, feta, Parmesan & dill. Add baking mix and stir to moisten. Spread evenly into 8 x 8 buttered pan. Bake for 30-35 minutes.

HOT CRAB APPETIZER

Judy Craig

8 oz. cream cheese
1 can (7 ½ oz.) drained crab meat
2 T. finely chopped onion

2 T. milk
½ t. creamed horseradish
¼ t. salt & pepper
½ c. toasted sliced almonds

Combine softened cream cheese, crab meat, onion, milk, horseradish and salt and pepper. Mix well until blended. Spoon into 9 inch pie plate and sprinkle with almonds. Bake at 375° for 15 - 20 minutes (needs to be very hot). Serve with crackers and spreader.

PARSONAGE PUNCH

Nina Freeman

2 (18 oz.) cans, unsweetened pineapple juice
3 c. orange juice
½ c. lemon juice
½ c. honey

2 (28 oz.) bottles, chilled ginger ale
3 pt. pineapple sherbet ice cream

Pour liquid together into a large punch bowl in the order listed. Carefully add ginger ale by pouring down the side of the bowl to avoid over flowing. Drop by spoon full of sherbet on top of the punch. Stir gently. Serves 32 small cups,

SHRIMP SALAD WITH ENDIVE

Nina Freeman

1 c. small shrimp (cooked)
½ c. mayonnaise
½ tsp. Dijon mustard

1 tsp. white wine
2 T. fresh dill
2 T chopped Chives

In a bowl, whisk together all ingredients. Add washed and dried shrimp. Serve with crackers or on endive.

ZUCCHINI APPETIZERS

Virginia Manchester

3 c. zucchini, grated
1 c. Bisquick
½ c. onion, chopped
½ c. Parmesan cheese, grated
2 T. parsley
½ tsp oregano

½ tsp salt
dash pepper
1 clove garlic, minced
¼ c. oil
4 eggs, beaten

Mix all ingredients and pour into 11x16 greased pan. Bake at 350° for 25 minutes, until golden brown. Cut into 48 squares.

263841-14

The first church building completed
in 1869 on East Miner

Soups
& Salads

Helpful Hints

- If the soup is not intended as the main course, count on 1 quart to serve 6. As the main dish, plan on 1 quart to serve 2.

- After cooking vegetables, pour any water and leftover vegetable pieces into a freezer container. When full, add tomato juice and seasoning to create a money-saving "free soup."

- Instant potatoes help thicken soups and stews.

- A leaf of lettuce dropped in a pot of soup absorbs grease from the top – remove the lettuce and serve. You can also make soup the day before, chill, and scrape off the hardened fat that rises to the top.

- To cut down on odors when cooking cabbage or cauliflower, add a little vinegar to the water and don't overcook.

- Three large stalks of celery, chopped and added to about two cups of beans (navy, brown, pinto, etc.), make the dish easier to digest.

- Fresh is best, but to reduce time in the kitchen, use canned or frozen broths or bouillon bases. Canned or frozen vegetables, such as peas, green beans, and corn, also work well.

- Ideally, cold soups should be served in chilled bowls.

- Perk up soggy lettuce by spritzing it with a mixture of lemon juice and cold water.

- You can easily remove egg shells from hard-boiled eggs if you quickly rinse the eggs in cold water after they are boiled. Add a drop of food coloring to help distinguish cooked eggs from raw ones.

- Your fruit salads will look better when you use an egg slicer to make perfect slices of strawberries, kiwis, or bananas.

- The ratio for a vinaigrette is typically 3 parts oil to 1 part vinegar.

- For salads, cook pasta al dente (slightly chewy to the bite). This allows the pasta to absorb some of the dressing and not become mushy.

- Fresh vegetables require little seasoning or cooking. If the vegetable is old, dress it up with sauces or seasoning.

- Chill the serving plates to keep the salad crisp.

- Fruit juices, such as pineapple and orange, can be used as salad dressing by adding a little olive oil, nutmeg, and honey.

SOUPS & SALADS

CALIFORNIA SALAD
Mary Klevan

1 c. pineapple chunks, drained
1 c. mandarin oranges. drained
1 c. shredded coconut

8 - 10 marshmallows, quartered
1 c. sour cream

Combine all ingredients in large bowl and refrigerate for 24 hours. Serve by placing a large portion on crisp lettuce cups.

COLD VERMICELLI SALAD
Fran Rudisill

1 pkg. vermicelli
2 T. olive oil
1 c. Girads Champagne
   Dressing
¼ tsp. dried basil

¾ c. mayonnaise
2 T. shredded gr. onion
2 T. parsley flakes
¼ tsp. oregano
2 T. red wine vinegar

Cook vermicelli in water and olive oil, drain. Toss with Champagne Dressing. Add rest of ingredients, and chill overnight.

CREAMY WILD RICE SOUP
Terri Joerg

¼ c. chopped onion
6 T. butter
6 T. flour
¼ tsp. salt
⅛ tsp. pepper
¼ Dijon mustard

1 can chicken broth
2 c. cooked wild rice
4 oz. can sliced mushrooms
¼ c. sherry
1 c. half & half

Sauté onion, stir in flour, salt, pepper, and mustard. Cover and cook until bubbly, gradually adding chicken broth. Heat until boiling, stirring constantly. Boil and stir one minute. Stir in wild rice, mushrooms, sherry, and half & half. Heat thoroughly. Do not boil. Serves 4-6 Manitok Indian recipe. Best with wild rice from Cherokee Indians in MINN. Hand collected from rivers and streams in northern MINN by canoe.

HAMBURGER SOUP

Jan Thanas

2 lb. ground beef
2 T. olive oil
½ tsp. salt
¼ tsp. pepper
¼ tsp. each basil and oregano
⅛ tsp. savory salt
1 pkg onion soup mix
6 c. boiling water

1 8 oz. can tomato sauce
1 T. soy sauce
1 c. celery, sliced
¼ c. carrots sliced
⅓ c dried split peas
1 c. elbow macaroni
Parmesan cheese

In large kettle with lid, brown meat in oil. Add salt and pepper, oregano, basil, savory salt and onion soup mix. Stir in boiling water, tomato sauce, and soy sauce. Cover and simmer 15 minutes. Add celery, carrots, celery leaves, add to simmering mixture. Continue to cook 30 minutes. Add spit peas and macaroni. Simmer 30 minutes. Add more water if necessary. Sprinkle grated cheese over individual servings. Serves 6-8.

HEARTY CABBAGE BEAN SOUP

Susie Freas

8 oz. turkey kielbasa, sliced
1 tsp. salt
1 T. oil
1 medium onion, chopped
1 small cabbage thinly sliced

½ tsp. thyme
¼ tsp. pepper
1 lg. can crushed tomatoes
1 can cannelloni beans
2 c. water

In large sauce pan, brown kielbasa in oil. Remove sausage from pan, reserving 1 T. oil. Salute onion, add herbs, then cabbage, sausage, tomatoes, and water. Simmer until cooks, about 20 minutes. Stir in drained beans last 5 minutes.

HODGE PODGE SOUP

Fran Rudisill

1 ½ hamburger
1 clove garlic
¾ c. onion
1 T. 3 e. Worcestershire

1 lg can pork & beans
3 cans minestrone soup
1 ½ c. chopped celery
½ tsp. oregano

Brown hamburger, garlic, and onions. Add rest of ingredients. Simmer until celery is cooked. (Your family/guests will think you spent hours in the kitchen). Very hearty!

263841-14

JOY'S CHICKEN SALAD

Joy Fagler

8 cooked chicken breast, cubed
6 stalks of celery, chopped
½ lg. red onion, chopped
1 lg. bunch of red grapes
1 10 oz. can of whole cashews

Dressing:
1¼ c. mayonnaise
½ tsp. curry powder
1-2 T. soy sauce
salt and pepper

Mix the first four ingredients in large salad bowl. Make dressing and mix into the salad. Refrigerate for 8 hours, stirring a couple of times during the day. Add cashews before serving.

LENTIL SOUP

Tony Waltman

2 celery stalks, diced
1 onion diced
1 cube unsalted butter
3 ham shanks
2 T. minced garlic
1 bag lentil (soak overnight in water)

black pepper to taste
seasoning salt to taste
Italian seasoning
1 cartons of Swanson's chicken broth
1 carton Farfalle pasta

In a large pot, sauté together butter, celery, onions, garlic. Add pepper, salt, and seasonings. Cook until celery and onion are translucent. Add broth, lentils, and ham. Cook for 1½ hour. Reduce heat to low, and remove ham bone. Trim meat from bone, returning ham to lentil mix, continue cooking for 30 minutes. Prepare pasta according to directions. We serve the pasta and soup together in a large soup bowl, topped with Parmesan cheese. I often use ham available from Holiday Dinner leftovers.

ORANGE MANDARIN AND LETTUCE SALAD

Nina Freeman

1 can mandarin oranges (drained)
2 c. celery, sliced
green onions, diced
grated carrots
1 bag of butter and red leaf lettuce

small bag sliced almonds
Dressing: ¼ c. vegetable oil
1 T. chopped parsley
2 T. sugar
2 T. vinegar
2 T. orange juice
dash of Tabasco

Mix lettuce, oranges, celery, onions, and carrots, then chill. Mix dressing ingredients in a glass jar. Lightly brown almonds with 3 T. sugar over low heat until browned. Dress chilled salad with mixed dressing, Garnish salad with almonds.

POTATO SOUP

Terri Joerg

1 30 oz. bag frozen hash brown potatoes
2 14 oz. cans chicken broth
1 can cream chicken soup

⅓ tsp. pepper
½ c. chopped onion
1 8 oz. fat free cream cheese
3 stalks green onion (minced)

In a crock pot, combine potatoes, broth, soup, onion and pepper. Cover and cook on low for 5 hours. Stir in room temperature cream cheese, cook 30 minutes, stirring until blended. Serve and garnish with green onion. Diced ham may be added.

RASPBERRY JELLO SALAD

Jacque Wallingford

2 (3-oz) pkgs. raspberry jello
1½ c. boiling water
1 lg. package frozen raspberries, thawed

1 can crushed pineapple (drained)
2 ripe bananas, mashed
½ pint sour cream

Dissolve jello in boiling water. Cool slightly. Add raspberries, pineapple, and bananas. Put ½ jello mixture in (11x13) pan. Let this set (approx 1 hour) and spread sour cream on top of jello mixture. Put the rest of jello on top of sour cream, and chill. Serve plain or with whipped cream. Options: May use strawberries rather than raspberries, This is a traditionally served at Thanksgiving with our family.

RASPBERRY MOLDED SALAD

Sharon Ehrenkranz
Susie Freas

1 6 oz. raspberry Jello
2 c. boiling water
1 pint vanilla ice cream

1 6 oz, pink lemonade
1 10 oz. frozen raspberries

Dissolve Jello in water. Stir in vanilla ice cream, one tablespoon at a time. Add lemonade and juice from thawed raspberries. When partially set, fold in raspberries. Chill completely. Great served with Breakfast Casserole and Spinach Salad, as a Spring/ Easter Brunch!

SATURDAY BEAN SOUP

Helen Holt

1 lb. dry navy beans (sort and soak overnite)
2 qt. water
1 lb. meaty ham bones
1 stalk celery, chopped

1 lg. carrot finely chopped
1 med. onion finely chopped
½ tsp. pepper
1 tsp. salt (optional)
1 bay leaf (optional)

(continued)

263841-14

Drain soaked beans, rinse, and put into crock pot with rest of ingredients. Cover and cook 5-6 hour on high. Lower temperature, and remove bay leaf. De-bone and cut ham into pieces. Heat for ½ to 1 hour. Freezes well.

SOUP OF SPRINGTIME

E J Sugar

4 T. butter
4 sm. leeks, only the white, finely chopped
1 sm. onion, finely chopped
1 small bunch carrots, (remove tops), peel and dice
1 sm. bunch asparagus, cut into 1" pieces, tops reserved
2 c. sm. red potatoes, peeled and chopped

4 c. low sodium chicken stock
2 c. fresh baby spinach, chopped coarsely
½ c. whole milk
2 T. flour
½ c. cream
salt and pepper to taste

In a large pot, sauté the onion and leeks in butter, until soft, but not browned. Add carrots, asparagus without tops, potatoes, and stock. Cook at a good simmer for 10-15 minutes until carrots are tender. Then add asparagus tops and spinach. Mix the flour in the milk to form a slurry, be careful to have no lumps, strain if necessary. Add to the soup, stirring carefully and let come to a boil. Add the cream and season to taste with salt and pepper.

SPINACH SALAD & DRESSING

Laurie Zamiska

spinach, washed and torn into pieces
bacon bits
chopped hard boiled eggs
sunflower seeds
alfalfa sprouts (fresh)
water chestnuts, sliced
croûtons

mushrooms, sliced
DRESSING: ½ c. wine vinegar
1 c. salad dressing
1 T. poppy seeds
½ c. sugar
1 tsp. salt
1 T. dry mustard
1 T. minced onions

Prepare dressing in a blender or small food processor. Mix thoroughly, set aside. Remove stems from spinach, tear spinach into bite size pieces (halves). Top salad with chopped eggs, bacon bits, water chestnuts, sunflower seeds, mushrooms, sprouts, and croûtons. Toss.

TEXAS CAVIAR (BEAN SALAD)

Terri Joerg

Salad: 1 can kidney beans
1 can black beans
1 can black eyed peas
1 can shoepeg corn
1 green pepper diced
1 medium onion diced

pimientos (I don't use any)
Dressing: ¾ c. cider vinegar
½ tsp. sugar
1 T. water
¾-1 c. sugar
¼ c. vegetable oil

Rinse beans and peas well. Drain corn. Mix all ingredients lightly. Bring ingredients to a boil, let cool slightly, then pour over bean mixture. Refrigerate for a few hours before serving. Keeps well for about a week.

263841-14

The second church building, erected in 1910,
at corner of Park and Hunter Streets

Vegetables
& Side Dishes

Helpful Hints

- When preparing a casserole, make an additional batch to freeze for when you're short on time. Use within 2 months.

- To keep hot oil from splattering, sprinkle a little salt or flour in the pan before frying.

- To prevent pasta from boiling over, place a wooden spoon or fork across the top of the pot while the pasta is boiling.

- Boil all vegetables that grow above ground without a cover.

- Never soak vegetables after slicing; they will lose much of their nutritional value.

- Green pepper may change the flavor of frozen casseroles. Clove, garlic, and pepper flavors get stronger when frozen, while sage, onion, and salt become more mild.

- For an easy no-mess side dish, grill vegetables along with your meat.

- Store dried pasta, rice (except brown rice), and whole grains in tightly covered containers in a cool, dry place. Refrigerate brown rice and freeze grains if you will not use them within 5 months.

- A few drops of lemon juice added to simmering rice will keep the grains separated.

- When cooking greens, add a teaspoon of sugar to the water to help vegetables retain their fresh colors.

- To dress up buttered, cooked vegetables, sprinkle them with toasted sesame seeds, toasted chopped nuts, canned french-fried onions, grated cheese, or slightly crushed seasoned croutons.

- Soufflé dishes are designed with straight sides to help your soufflé rise. Ramekins work well for single-serve casseroles.

- A little vinegar or lemon juice added to potatoes before draining will make them extra white when mashed.

- To avoid toughened beans or corn, add salt midway through cooking.

- If your pasta sauce seems a little dry, add a few tablespoons of the pasta's cooking water.

- To prevent cheese from sticking to a grater, spray the grater with cooking spray before beginning.

VEGETABLES & SIDE DISHES

ANDERSON'S GREEN BEAN DISH

Judy Craig

6 cans French Style green beans (drained)
2 c. toasted almonds slices
1 c. bread crumbs
2 cans cream of mushroom soup

1 small size of Velveeta cheese cubed
1½ T. Worcestershire sauce
2 tsp. garlic salt
1 tsp. chile powder
6 drops of Tabasco sauce

To make sauce, add cream of mushroom soup, cheese, worcestershire sauce, garlic salt, chile powder and Tabasco sauce. Cook slowly, stir until everything is melted. In large casserole dish, put 2 of the well drained cans of bean, spread evenly, sprinkle ⅓ of the almonds over the beans and cover that with ⅓ of the sauce. Repeat this two more times and then cover with bread crumbs and dot with butter. Bake at 350°, for 1 hour and has 8 servings.

BROCCOLI CASSEROLE

Virginia Manchester

2 beaten eggs
1 c. mayonnaise
1 c. grated cheddar cheese

1 can celery soup
2 pkg frozen broccoli
2 T. chopped onion

Mix all ingredients and put in casserole dish. Bake at 350° for 30 to 40 minutes until broccoli is cooked. Top casserole with 1 cup cracker crumbs and ½ cup mayonnaise. Cooke at 450° for 10 minutes or until crumbs are brown.

CALIFORNIA QUICHE

Judy Craig

1 c. mushrooms, chopped
½ c. celery, chopped
½ c. green onions, chopped
2 T. butter
6 eggs
1½ c. milk
¼ c. flour
1 tsp. salt

1 tsp. paprika
⅛ tsp. hot sauce
½ c. cooked bacon
½ c. cooked sausage
1 c. Swiss cheese, graded
1 c. cheddar cheese, graded
1 T. white wine

Sauté the chopped items in butter and set aside. Beat eggs, then add flour salt, paprika and hot sauce. Then add all the ingredients together and refrigerate for 12 hours. Pour mixture into a greased quiche pan or pie pan and bake at 350° for 45 or 50 minutes. Let quiche set for 15 minutes before serving.

CANNELONI WITH TWO CHEESES

Diane Fender

8 manicotti shells
1 pkg. frozen spinach
⅛ tsp. pepper
2 T. lemon juice
8 oz. can tomato sauce
½ c. Monterey Jack cheese, grated

½ tsp. salt
¼ tsp. nutmeg
1 pt. small curd cottage cheese
¼ c. instant minced onions
½ tsp. basil, well crumbled
Herb Sauce (see below)

Drop shells into boiling water, simmer for 5 minutes. Drain carefully. Defrost spinach and drain thoroughly. Mix spinach, cottage cheese, minced onion, basil, salt, nutmeg, pepper & lemon juice. Stuff into parboiled shells. Pour half of Herb Sauce (see below)in baking dish; placing filled shells in single layer on sauce. Cover completely with remaining sauce. Pour tomato sauce in strips over filled shells. Sprinkle with cheese. Cover with foil and bake at 350 for 45 minutes. Herb Sauce: ¼ c. butter, 1 clove minced garlic, 1 t. salt, 2 T. parsley, 3 T. flour, 1 t. basil and 2 c. milk. Melt butter and stir in flour, garlic, basil and salt. Add milk and cook over medium heat until thickened and boiling. Stir in parsley

CARROT & ZUCCHINI MEDLEY

Jan Thanas

2 T. butter or margarine
1 lg. onion, thinly sliced
1 lb. carrots, cut in ¼ thick slices
1 lb. zucchini, cut in ¼ thick slices

1 T. chopped parsley
¾ tsp. salt
¾ tsp. savory

Melt butter in wide frying pan on medium heat. Add onion, stirring occasionally until limp & golden (about 15 min.). Add carrots & cook for 3 min., then add zucchini & cook additional 5 min. Stirring occasionally until vegetables are crisp & tender. Stir in parsley, salt & savory. Serves ⅚ people

CREAM CHEESE PASTA SAUCE

Diane Fender

2 c. broth
8 oz. cream cheese
1 clove garlic, crushed

¼ c. Parmesan cheese
basil to taste

Stir over heat until blended the first 3 ingredients. Then add the last 2 ingredients and serve over cooked pasta.

263841-14

CROCK POT BEANS

Helen Holt

1 lb. hamburger
1 lb. bacon -cut in pieces
1 c. chopped onions
2 cans (1 lb.) pork & beans
1 can kidney beans
1 can cut green beans

1 c. ketchup
¼ c. brown sugar
½ T. liquid smoke
3 T. white vinegar
1 t. salt
dash of pepper

Brown the first three ingredients together and drain off any liquid. Mix the remaining ingredients into a crock pot and cook on low for 4 to 9 hours

KUGLE

Marlene Guilliano
Susie Freas

1 bag wide egg noodles.
1 pint sour cream
1 pint cottage cheese

¼ lb. butter
3 eggs- scrambled
dash of nutmeg

Mix the above ingredients together. Pour into 9'x13" greased pan. Lightly sprinkle nutmeg over top of casserole. Bake at 425° for 20 minutes, then lower to 350° until golden brown. .

LEEKS AND CREAMED PEAS

Jeri Ross

4 lg leeks
1 ½ c. whipping cream
2 T. butter

1 pkg. frozen peas
Salt & pepper to taste

Cut leeks in half, lengthwise, then slice cross wise in ¼ inch pieces, from white end to beginning of dark green stalks. Melt butter in frying pan on medium heat. Add leeks and cook for 3 or 4 minutes, until wilted. Add cream, salt and pepper. Simmer until tender, about 10 minutes, add peas and cook until peas are done.

MARINARA SAUCE

Diane Fender

3 onions, chopped
3 ribs celery, chopped
3 zucchini, chopped
½ bottle dry red wine
5 cloves garlic, crushed

10 fresh tomatoes, chopped
1 c. sliced mushrooms
oregano, salt and bay leaf
oil

Brown onions, celery and garlic in oil. Add remaining ingredients and spices to taste. Simmer for 1 - 3 hours.

MOM'S STUFFED CABBAGE

Regina Brown

1 lb. ground beef
½ lb. ground pork
salt to taste
1 t. paprika
½ t. black pepper
1 T. minced parsley or celery
    leaves

½ c. uncooked rice
1 med onion - chopped
1 large head of cabbage
2 c. sauerkraut
3 c. tomato juice
1 c. water
sour cream, if desired

Core cabbage and place in enough boiling water to cover. With a fork in one hand and a knife in the other, keep cutting off the leaves, as they become wilted. Drain. Trim the thick center vein of each cabbage leaf. In large bowl, add meat, seasonings, onion, water and rice. Mix well. Place a tablespoon of filling mixture on each cabbage leaf and roll, and tucking in edges. Alternate sauerkraut and cabbage rolls in layers, beginning with sauerkraut on large pot. Cover ⅔ full with water and then add tomato juice. Cover and simmer for about 2 hours or until rice is done. When the cabbage rolls are done, brown a cube of butter and pour over the cabbage rolls. Mix it in and serve with sour cream on top. Serves 8 people

VEGETABLE MEDLEY - SWEDISH SALAD

Terri Joerg

1 - 16 oz can Le Sueur Peas,
    drained
1 - 16 oz can white shoe peg
    corn
1 - 16 oz french style green
    beans

Pimento
1 c. chopped celery
1 green pepper, chopped
1 c. chopped purple onion

Combine all ingredients and bring to a boil. Cool these ingredients. Add dressing and refrigerate for 8 hours. Dressing: 1 cup sugar, ½ cup vinegar, ½ cup oil, 1 t. salt, 1 t. pepper.

WALDORF SALAD

Tony Waltman

1 pkg. Greens, romaine or
    mixed baby greens
2 c. celery, chopped
2 c. seedless red grapes, cut in
    half

2 c. skinned and sliced apple
1 pkg. blue cheese or
    Gorgonzola cheese crumbles
1 c. candied walnuts
Balsamic Dressing

Candied Walnuts: In large sauce pan, heat 2 T. butter and 1 c. sugar, until mixture is like a brown syrup. Remove from heat and add 2 cups walnut halves and mix well. Pour on cookie sheet that has been sprayed

(continued)

with Pam. Once cooled, break apart walnuts. Once walnuts are cooled, mix all ingredients in large salad bowl and serve. You can also keep ingredients separate and let people mix their own salad.

ZUCCHINI RICE CASSEROLE
Nancy Huff

1½ lb. zucchini - sliced
¾ to 1 c. grated Swiss cheese
½ c. uncooked rice
1 can cream of mushroom soup
1 c. water

1 small can sliced mushrooms
1 t. salt
¼ t. pepper
2 sliced bacon

Arrange in layers: zucchini, rice, mushrooms, cheese and mixture of soup and water. Top with bacon slices and more cheese. Bake for 1 hour at 350°, uncovered.

VEGETABLES & SIDE DISHES

Willow Street, our third church,
was site of many great potlucks.

Main Dishes

263841-sg-4m

Helpful Hints

- Certain meats, like ribs and pot roast, can be parboiled before grilling to reduce the fat content.

- Pound meat lightly with a mallet or rolling pin, pierce with a fork, sprinkle lightly with meat tenderizer, and add marinade. Refrigerate for 20 minutes and cook or grill for a quick and succulent meat.

- Marinating is a cinch if you use a plastic bag. The meat stays in the marinade and it's easy to turn. Cleanup is easy; just toss the bag.

- It's easier to thinly slice meat if it's partially frozen.

- Adding tomatoes to roasts naturally tenderizes the meat as tomatoes contain an acid that works well to break down meats.

- Whenever possible, cut meat across the grain; this will make it easier to eat and also give it a more attractive appearance.

- When frying meat, sprinkle paprika on the meat to turn it golden brown.

- Thaw all meats in the refrigerator for maximum safety.

- Refrigerate poultry promptly after purchasing. Keep it in the coldest part of your refrigerator for up to 2 days. Freeze poultry for longer storage. Never leave poultry at room temperature for over 2 hours.

- When frying chicken, canola oil provides a milder taste, and it contains healthier amounts of saturated and polyunsaturated fats. Do not cover the chicken once it has finished cooking because covering will cause the coating to lose its crispness.

- One pound of boneless chicken equals approximately 3 cups of cubed chicken.

- Generally, red meats should reach 160° and poultry should reach 180° before serving. If preparing fish, the surface of the fish should flake off with a fork.

- Rub lemon juice on fish before cooking to enhance the flavor and help maintain a good color.

- Scaling a fish is easier if vinegar is rubbed on the scales first.

- When grilling fish, the rule of thumb is to cook 5 minutes on each side per inch of thickness. For example, cook a 2-inch thick fillet for 10 minutes per side. Before grilling, rub with oil to seal in moisture.

MAIN DISHES

AUNT OLGA'S RISSOLES

Aunt Olga
Cindy Green

1 lb. hamburger
1 c. mashed potatoes
1 onion - finely chopped
1 large tomato - finely chopped

1 egg yolk
dash of salt
olive oil
flour (for gravy)

In large bowl combine the first 6 ingredients and mix gently. Shape into "golf ball size" meatballs. Fry these in a small amount of olive oil and place in small pan and keep warm. Brown flour in remaining oil and make a gravy. Pour gravy over cooked meat balls.

BARBEQUE BEEF SANDWICHES

Terri Joerg

3 (lb.) beef chuck roast
1 tsp. salt
½ tap. pepper
1 lg. onion, chopped
1 c. celery stalk and leaves, chopped
1 tsp. garlic salt
1 tsp. chili powder
1 bay leaf
SAUCE: 1 minced clove garlic
2 med. onions chopped
¼ c. oleo

¼ c. brown sugar
2 c. canned tomatoes
⅛ tsp. red pepper
1 tsp. prepared mustard
1 c. liquid from meat
¼ c. lemon juice
¼ c. vinegar
1 (8 oz.) canned tomato purée paste
2 tsp. chili powder
1 cup chopped celery

In a big pan; add water to 1" above meat. Add rest of ingredients. Bring to a rapid boil. Simmer 2-3 hours. Pour ½ the liquid from the pan, saving the remaining liquid. Cool, then shred meat, discarding gristle and fat. Put in 3 quart (shallow) baking dish. To prepare sauce, simmer all ingredients for 40 minutes. Pour over meat. Bake at 350° until most of liquid is absorbed. Serve over crusty rolls. Serves 12-15

BEEF AND NOODLE CASSEROLE

Laurie Zamiska

4 lbs. ground beef (or ground turkey)
3 12 oz. pkgs fine noodles
4 cans mushroom soup

½ c. onion, chopped
salt or seasoned salt to taste
½ lb. butter or margarine (melted)

(continued)

Brown beef and onion in about 1 tablespoon butter. Cook slowly until meat is well done. Add cooked, drained noodles. Stirring with a fork add mushrooms and butter. Bake at 350° for 30 minutes. Serves 25 Recipe may be divided into ⅓ or ½. Kids love this dish!

BREAKFAST CASSEROLE

Mimi Ronaldson
Susie Freas

1 lb. breakfast sausage, cooked
1 lb. grated Cheddar cheese
12 eggs
1 tsp. dry mustard
salt & pepper

4 green onions, chopped
½ green pepper, chopped
1 sm. box mushrooms, sliced
6 slices white bread, without crusts.

Cover bottom of a 9"x13" buttered pan, with white bread. Spread sausage and Cheddar cheese over bread. Beat eggs, milk, mustard, salt and pepper. Pour over meat and cheese. Top with green onions, mushrooms, and green pepper. Cover tightly and refrigerate overnite, Bake uncovered 300° for about 1 ½ hours.

BROCCOLI MUSHROOM QUICHE

Susie Freas

1 broccoli, small head cut into flowerette size pieces
4-5 mushrooms sliced
½ T. garlic powder
½ tsp. salt
½ tsp. pepper
¾ tsp .oregano

1 9 in. deep pie crust.
4 oz. Swiss cheese, cut into small cubes
4 eggs
1 c. 2 or 4 % milk
1 c cream

Pre-bake pie shell at 375° for 10 minutes. Lower oven to 350° Sauté onions and broccoli, adding mushrooms near end of cook time. Place cheese into still warm shell, adding vegetables. Beat eggs, add milk, cream, and seasonings. Pour egg mixture until ½" from rim. Bake quiche until top is lightly browned and a knife inserted into center comes out clean, 40-50 minutes.

CHICKEN DRESSING CASSEROLE

Patty Pinnick

2 or 3 cooked chicken breast
2 cans cream of chicken soup
2 cans chicken broth

1 10 oz. package frozen peas
½ c. minute rice
1 box of stove top dressing

(continued)

Prepare the box of stove top dressing. Put aside. Cut up chicken breast and place in a 9 X 13 inch casserole that has been sprayed with non-stick cooking spray. Heat up the cans of soup and add the package of peas and rice. Pour over the chicken and the cover with the prepared stove top dressing. Bake for 325° minutes for 30 minutes.

CHICKEN DIVAN
Susie Freas

4 lg. chicken breasts lightly poached
2 boxes of frozen broccoli spears, steamed al dente
2 cans cream of mushroom soup

5 T. mayonnaise
Seasoned breadcrumbs
1 lg. bag of shredded cheddar cheese

Arrange chicken pieces and broccoli in pan. Layer with sauce, if using a smaller casserole dish. Mix soup with mayonnaise, pour over chicken and broccoli. Top with cheese, then bread crumbs. Dot with butter. Bake at 350° for 1 hour, or until bubbling and slightly brown.

CHICKEN RICE CASSEROLE
June Davies

1 ¼ c. uncooked rice
½ c. chopped onions
1 can cream of mushroom soup
1 can cream of chicken soup

1 can cream of celery soup
¼ c. melted margarine
10 chicken thighs

Place chicken thighs in large casserole. Mix the rest of the ingredients and pour over the chicken thighs. Dot with ½ cup of margarine. Bake for 2 ½ to 3 hours at 250°.

CHILI RELLENO CASSEROLE
Nina Freeman

1 can whole green chilies
1 4 oz. can chopped chilles
1 c. Bisquick
3 eggs
1 c. milk

½ tsp. salt
½ lb. grated Monterey Jack cheese
½ lb. grated Cheddar cheese

Preheat oven to 350° Rinse and split whole chilies in half. Mix together well, Bisquick, eggs, milk, and salt, Mix cheeses, set aside. Put ½ Bisquick mix on bottom of greased baking dish. Top with whole chilies and ½ cheese. Repeat by pouring remaining batter, then chilies and cheese. Bake 40-45 minutes at 350°.

CORN AND CHEESE CHOWDER

Nina Freeman

¼ pound sliced bacon cut in eighths
1 medium onion chopped
½ c, celery chopped
¼ c. celery leaves chopped
½ c. green pepper chopped
½ bay leaf

1 12 oz.can corn
3 c. milk
1½ tsp. seasoned salt
⅛ tsp. white pepper
1½ c. shredded Monterey Jack cheese

Using a large pot, fry bacon until crisp. Remove bacon and save for garnish. Add onion, celery, celery leaves, green pepper, and bay leaf to bacon drippings. Sauté 8 minutes or until crisp and tender. Mix in flour and undrained corn, milk, salt and pepper. Cook over medium heat until soup comes to a boil and is slightly thickened, stirring constantly. Just before serving add cheese and garnish with bacon pieces.

EASY PARMESAN GARLIC CHICKEN

Nina Freeman

½ c. Parmesan cheese
1 envelope Good Seasonings Italian Dressing

6 boneless chicken breast halves
½ tsp. garlic powder

Mix cheese, salad seasonings mix, and garlic powder. Moisten chicken with water. Coat with cheese mixture. Place in shallow baking dish which has been coated with cooking spray. Bake at 400 for 20 to 25 minutes, or until chicken is cooked through. Serves 6

GREEK-STYLE CHICKEN

Jan Thanas

15 double crackers
3½ to 4 lb. chicken pieces
⅓ c. lemon juice
⅓ c. lime juice
½ t. dried thyme

1 clove garlic, minced
1 t. salt
¼ t. pepper
⅓ c. dry white wine
¼ to ½ c. melted butter

Crush crackers into fine crumbs and set aside. Place chicken in marinade of lemon juice, lime juice, thyme, garlic, salt, pepper and wine. Let stand for 3 hours, turning at least once. Drain chicken and save the marinade. Roll each piece of chicken in crumbs and place in shallow baking pan. Drizzle with butter. Bake in 350° oven for 45 minutes or until done. Baste with marinade about twice during baking. Serves 8

ITALIAN DELIGHT

Sally Carson
June Davies

½ lb. spaghetti
2 small onions
1 bell pepper chopped)
2 lb. ground beef
1 can pitted olives
2 cans tomato sauce
2 cans water
1 sm. can mushrooms (drained)

½ lb. grated cheese
1 can whole kernel corn
Seasonings: ½ tsp. each cumin,
   oregano, salt, poultry
   seasoning, black pepper
1 T. paprika, chili powder,
   Worcestershire sauce
¼ tsp. garlic sauce

Brown meat in oil and add chopped onion and green pepper. Add all other ingredients and seasonings. Cook spaghetti, drain. Add to beef mixture. Bake at 325° for approximately 1 hour. Serves 14 ("But not if you invite the Carson family!" says Sally)

JOHN WAYNE'S CHILI RELLENOS

Jeff Hopson

3 4 oz. cans green chili seeded
   (whole or chopped)
1 lb. Monterrey Jack cheese
1 lb. Cheddar cheese

4 eggs
½ c. flour
1 ½ c. milk

Mix both cheeses. In 2 ½ quart casserole dish, layer chili, then cheese for 3 layers. Beat eggs, add milk and flour. Pour this mixture over layers of chili and cheese and bake for 1 hour at 350°. Serve hot. My Dad had the opportunity to work with the Duke, when he bought a Grand Champion Bull from Oxley Ranch in Oaklahoma.

LETTUCE WRAPS

E J Sugar

6 oz. lean ground meat(turkey,
   chicken, or pork)
1 small onion, chopped
½ c. mushrooms, chopped
1 T. extra light olive oil
½ c. water chestnuts, chopped
½ c. carrots, grated (optional)
lettuce leaves (Bibb, Boston,
   butter or romaine)
Meat Marinade:

½ tsp. salt
½ tsp. sugar
2 tsp.. cornstarch
Seasoning Sauce:
2 T. chicken broth
1 tsp. cornstarch
1 T. soy sauce
1 T. oyster sauce
¼ tsp. red pepper flakes
   (optional)

Combine the meat and marinade and let sit. Sauté the onion and mushrooms in olive oil until liquid is absorbed. Add the meat and cook 3 minutes or until the meat is no longer pink. Add the water chestnuts, carrots, and seasoning sauce and cook until heated through. Serve warm in lettuce leaves.

MACARONI IMPERIAL

Gramma Julia Davies
June Davies

1 cup uncooked macaroni,
  broken into 1 inch pieces
½ c. soft bread crumbs
3 T. red pepper finely chopped
¼ c. melted butter
3 T. green pepper, finely
  chopped

1½ tsp. chopped onion
1½ tsp. salt
1 c. grated American cheese
1½ c. scalded milk
3 egg yokes, well beaten
3 egg whites, stiffly beaten

Cook macaroni in large amount of salted boiling water until tender. Drain. Add bread crumbs, butter, red & green pepper, onions, salt and cheese. Add milk. Pour over beaten egg yolks, stirring well. Add macaroni, then fold in egg whites. Pour into well greased casserole; place into pan of hot water, and bake in moderate 350° oven, for 40-45 minutes, or firm. Serves 8

MEXICAN TORTILLA BAKE

Nina Freeman

2 lb. lean ground beef
1 onion chopped
1 clove garlic, minced
2 8 oz. cans tomato sauce
1-2 tsp. chili powder
¼ tsp. salt

½ c. sour cream
9 corn tortillas
2 c, shredded Monterey Jack
  cheese
1 can sliced olives

Brown meat with onions and garlic, in a shallow pan. Add tomato sauce, a little water, and chili powder. Simmer 20 minutes. Spread tortillas with meat sauce, cheese and sour cream. Continue layering meat sauce, tortillas, cheese and sour cream until all are used. Garnish with olives. Bake at 350° for 35-40 minutes.

ORZO WITH ROASTED VEGETABLES

Nina Freeman

1 sm. eggplant, peeled and
  diced into ¾" pieces
1 red bell pepper, diced
1 yellow bell pepper, diced
2 garlic cloves, minced
⅓ c. good olive oil
1½ tsp kosher salt
½ tsp. black pepper
½ lb orzo, or rice shaped pasta
⅓ c. freshly squeezed lemon
  juice (2 lemons)⅓ c. good
  olive oil

1 tsp. kosher salt
½ tsp. black pepper
4 scallions minced (white and
  green parts)
¼ c. pine nuts
¾ lb. Feta cheese, (½ inch
  diced)
15 fresh basil leaves

(continued)

263841-14

Preheat oven to 425° Toss eggplant, bell peppers, onion, garlic with our, salt, and pepper on a large sheet pan. Roast for 40 minutes, until browned, turning once with spatula. Meanwhile cook orzo in boiling water for 7-9 minutes. Drain and transfer to large serving bowl. Add roasted vegetables to pasta, scraping all liquid and seasonings from roasting pan into pasta bowl. Combine lemon juice, olive oil, salt and pepper, then pour on pasta and vegetables. Let cool to room temperature. Add scallions, pine nuts, feta, and basil. Check the seasonings and serve at room temperature.

OVEN STEW
Nancy Huff

2 lb. stew meat	salt and pepper
1 sliced onion	1 can consomme
¼ c. flour	½ c. red wine
¼ c. bread crumbs	1 can sliced mushrooms

Mix all ingredients together and place in a covered casserole. Bake for 3 hours at 300. Excellent with mashed potatoes or cooked noodles.

OVERNITE BARBECUED CHICKEN
Terri Joerg

2 broiler-fryer chickens, cut up	1½ c. catsup
2 inches water in big pot	2 tsp. salt
Marinade: ½ c. wine vinegar	1½ tsp. pepper
4 T. Worcestershire sauce	2½ T. dry mustard
½ c. water	2 tsp. paprika
1½ c. brown sugar	2 dashes Hot pepper sauce

Poach chicken in 2 inches of water for half an hour in a large covered pot, then drain. Combine marinade ingredients in a blender and whirl until thoroughly mixed. Reserve 1 cup of this mixture and let chicken stand overnight in the remainder of marinade. Grill chicken on barbecue until brown and crisp. While chicken is barbecuing, heat reserved marinade and simmer 5 minutes: serve with chicken,

PARMESAN CHEESE MEAT DISH
Mary Klevan

1 lb. ground beef	¼ tsp. pepper
½ c. soft bread crumbs	2 T. cooking oil
½ c. grated Parmesan cheese	¼ c. flour
1 slightly beaten egg	1 c. beef bouillon
½ c. milk	1 3 oz. can mushrooms
1 T. minced onion (dried)	(undrained)
½ tsp. salt	½ c. white wine

(continued)

Combine beef, bread crumbs, cheese, egg, milk, onion, salt and pepper. Shape into 12 balls and brown in hot oil. Remove from skillet. Blend flour into pan drippings; stir in flour, add bouillon, wine, and undrained mushrooms. Return meatballs to sauce, Cover and simmer about 30 minutes. Check often so they won't stick. Stir carefully. Delicious over rice.

PINEAPPLE CHICKEN

Nina Freeman

4 to 6 boneless skinless chicken
   breast
⅛ t. pepper
paprika to taste
1 can - 20 oz. pineapple tidbits,
   drained

2 T. Dijon mustard
2 to 3 T. soy sauce
¼ t. minced garlic

Place chicken in greased 3½ to 5 quart slow cooker. Sprinkle with pepper and paprika. In a separate bowl, mix pineapple tidbits, mustard, soy sauce and garlic together and pour over chicken. Cover and cook on high heat for 3-4 hours or on low heat for 7-9 hours. Makes 4 to 6 servings.

ROSSINI (SAUSAGE AND BROCCOLI PASTA)

Susie Freas

2 T. oil
3 cloves garlic, chopped
½ pint mushrooms, sliced
1 lb. mild Italian sausage, bulk,
   or removed from casing

parsley and oregano to taste
1 head broccoli tops,
1 can chicken broth
1 small box spaghetti

Brown sausage, adding broccoli tops, onion, mushrooms and garlic last five minutes. Cook until tender. Drain oil. Add herbs and chicken broth. Set aside. Cook spaghetti until tender, then drain. Plate pasta, topping with meat mixture.

SAUCY MEAT LOAF

Donna Schnor
Sherry Fisher

1 egg, slightly beaten
1½ t. salt
¼ c. chopped onion
¾ t. chile powder
1 T. Worcestershire sauce
1½ lbs. lean ground beef

2 T. catsup
1 c. Quick Oats
¼ c. chopped onion
½ c. milk
Topping: 4 T. catsup and 1 T.
   brown sugar

(continued)

263841-14

Combine all ingredients and mix well. Shape into loaf and place in a shallow pan. Bake at 350 for about 1 hour. Combine topping ingredients and spread over meat. Bake at 350 for 15 minutes.

SESAME CHICKEN
Susie Freas

8 boneless, skinless chicken
  breast halves
½ c. buttermilk
2 tsp. thyme

¾-1 c. breadcrumbs
salt & pepper to taste
¾ c. sesame seeds

Preheat oven to 400° (You may want to toast sesame seeds in your preheating oven. Place seeds in baking dish, set in oven, stirring occasionally until golden brown, about 15 minutes). Arrange chicken on a wide dinner plate, pour buttermilk over chicken, set aside. Combine thyme, with breadcrumbs, salt and pepper with sesame seeds. Generously coat a wide roasting pan with vegetable oil. Remove a chicken piece from plate, shake gently to remove drips, and place in crumbs. Coat completely pressing firmly with your fingers. Repeat with remaining chicken pieces. Sprinkle again with salt. Bake 15 minutes or until pieces are cooked through. Bone in thighs will take longer. Serve with mango chutney, rice, and broccoli. We use boneless thighs. Serves 4-6

SHRIMP SCAMPI
Vicki Alverson

1 c. white wine
½ c. unsalted butter
3 t. minced garlic

1 lb. shrimp, peeled and de-
  veined

Combine all ingredients and bake at 350° for 6 to 7 minutes. Be careful not to overcook the shrimp. Shrimp is done when it has turned pink.

SWEDISH MEATBALLS
E J Sugar

1 ½ lbs. ground beef
1 egg
½ c. whole milk
½ c. fresh bread crumbs
½ c. onion, chopped
4 T. butter, divided
2 tsp. sugar
1 tsp. salt
½ tsp. nutmeg

½ tsp. allspice
1 c. mushrooms, sliced
Gravy: 2 T. butter
3 T. flour
1 c. whole milk
1 c. water
1 tsp. salt
¼ tsp. pepper

Combine the egg, milk, bread crumbs, and spices in a large bowl. Set aside to soften. Meanwhile, sauté the onions in 2 tsp. butter until

(continued)

softened. Blend the beef and cooked onions well into the egg mixture. Form into balls and cook in the remaining butter, Place the cooked meatballs into a casserole. Using the drippings in the pan, sauté the mushrooms. Pour over the meatballs and set aside to make gravy. Cook the flour in the butter and stir in milk, water and seasonings. Simmer until thickened slightly. Add more milk if necessary because it will get thicker as it cooks. Pour the gravy over the meatballs and bake at 350° for 30 minutes. Serve with cooked noodles or mashed potatoes.

TACO LASAGNA

Nina Freeman

1 lb. ground turkey
½ c. green bell pepper, chopped
½ c. onion, chopped
⅔ c. water
1 envelope taco seasoning
1 15 oz. can black beans, rinsed

1 4 oz. can Mexican diced
  tomatoes
6 flour tortillas
1 can refried beans
3 c. shredded Mexican cheese
chopped fresh cilantro

Cook ground turkey, green pepper, and onion over medium heat until meat is no longer pink. Drain well. Add water and taco seasonings, then bring to a boil. Reduce heat, simmer 2 minutes. Stir in black beans and tomatoes. Simmer uncovered for 10 minutes, Place 2 tortillas in greased 9'x13' pan. Spread with ½ refried beans and meat mixture. Top with 1 c. cheese. Repeat layer, topping with remaining tortilla and cheese. Cover and bake at 350° for 25 minutes. Garnish with cilantro and serve with sour cream.

TALLARINES

Jan Thanas

1 6 oz. pkg. fine noodles
2 lb. ground beef
2 onions, chopped
2 cloves garlic, chopped
1 green pepper, chopped
2 T. oil

2 14 oz. cans tomatoes
1 12 oz. can corn
1 c. ripe olives
1 4 oz. can mushrooms
2 c. grated cheese
salt & pepper to taste

Cook noodles in salted water until tender and then drain off water. Sauté meat, onions, garlic and green pepper in oil until meat is browned. Add tomatoes, salt and pepper, then simmer for 10 minutes. Combine noodles, meat mixture and remaining ingredients, but save ½ c. cheese to sprinkle over top. Turn into a greased casserole dish and sprinkle with cheese. Bake at 350° for 1 hour.

263841-14

TAMALE PIE CASSEROLE
Sherry Fisher

1 ½ lbs. ground round
2 med. onions (chopped)
2 cloves garlic (crushed)
1 4 oz. can sliced mushrooms
1 med. green pepper (well chopped)
3 14 oz. cans tomato sauce

¼ c. water
1 T. chili powder
dash of hot sauce
salt & pepper
1 c. sliced olives
tortilla chips (small bag)
1 lb. grated cheddar cheese

Brown meat and drain off fat. Add onions and garlic and simmer for 5 minutes. Add remaining ingredients, except cheese and tortilla chips and cook for 30 minutes. Layer cooked mixture, chips and cheese in large casserole and repeat for a second layer. Bake for 30 minutes at 350°.

TURKEY PUFF SANDWICH
Jeff Hopson

1 can condensed milk
5 eggs
1 lb. sliced cooked turkey or chicken
8 slices of bread

1 T. chopped parsley
salt, pepper and poultry seasoning to taste
soft butter
1 c. mayonnaise

Spread mayonnaise on bread slices. Add turkey or chicken and season with salt, pepper, and poultry seasoning. Put on second slice of bread and spread with butter. Cut sandwiches on the diagonal. Mix condensed milk, eggs, and salt and pepper. Place cut sandwiches in baking dish and pour milk and eggs mixture over sandwiches. Put this dish into the refrigerator overnight. Bake at 350° for 60 to 70 minutes or until the sandwich dish is "puffed" and golden brown. Serve with cranberry relish. This is my VERY FAVORITE way to eat left over turkey, any time!

UN-STUFFED CABBAGE ROLLS
Terri Joerg

1 ½- 2 lb. ground beef
1 T. oil
1 large onion, chopped
1 clove garlic, minced
1 small cabbage, chopped

2 cans (14.5 oz,) diced tomatoes
1 can (8 0z.) tomato sauce
½ c. water
1 tsp. sea salt
1 tsp. pepper

Heat oil over medium heat. Add the ground beef and onion. Cook, stirring until beef is no longer pink, and onion is tender. Add garlic, continue cooking 1 minute. Add chopped cabbage, tomatoes, pepper and salt. Cover and simmer 20-30 minutes, until cabbage is tender. Serves 6-8 May serve with rice or quinoa.

MAIN DISHES

This stained glass angel has a new
home in our sanctuary.

Breads & Rolls

Helpful Hints

- When baking bread, a small dish of water in the oven will keep the crust from getting too hard or brown.

- Use shortening, not margarine or oil, to grease pans when baking bread. Margarine and oil absorb more readily into the dough.

- To make self-rising flour, mix 4 cups flour, 2 teaspoons salt, and 2 tablespoons baking powder. Store in a tightly covered container.

- One scant tablespoon of bulk yeast is equal to one packet of yeast.

- Hot water kills yeast. One way to test for the correct temperature is to pour the water over your wrist. If you cannot feel hot or cold, the temperature is just right.

- When in doubt, always sift flour before measuring.

- Use bread flour for baking heavier breads, such as mixed grain, pizza doughs, bagels, etc.

- When baking in a glass pan, reduce the oven temperature by 25°.

- When baking bread, you can achieve a finer texture if you use milk. Water makes a coarser bread.

- Fill an empty salt shaker with flour to quickly and easily dust a bread pan or work surface.

- For successful quick breads, do not overmix the dough. Mix only until combined. An overmixed batter creates tough and rubbery muffins, biscuits, and quick breads.

- Muffins can be eaten warm. Most other quick breads taste better the next day. Nut breads are better if stored 24 hours before serving.

- Nuts, shelled or unshelled, keep best and longest when stored in the freezer. Unshelled nuts crack more easily when frozen. Nuts can be used directly from the freezer.

- Enhance the flavor of nuts, such as almonds, walnuts, and pecans, by toasting them before using in recipes. Place nuts on a baking sheet and bake at 300° for 5−8 minutes or until slightly browned.

- Overripe bananas can be frozen until it's time to bake. Store them unpeeled in a plastic bag.

- The freshness of eggs can be tested by placing them in a large bowl of cold water; if they float, do not use them.

BREADS & ROLLS

CRANBERRY BREAD

Laurie Zamiska

2 c. flour
½ tsp. salt
½ tsp. soda
1½ tsp. baking powder
2 T. butter
1 c. sugar

1 egg, beaten slightly
juice of 1 orange
grated rind of orange
boiling water
1 c. whole cranberries
½ c. chopped walnuts

Sift all dry ingredients together. Dust cranberries and nuts with flour. Place juice and rind in measuring cup and add boiling water to make ¾ c. Blend butter and sugar until creamy, add slightly beaten egg, then orange juice mixture. Blend this with nuts and cranberries into dry ingredients. Place in greased, small loaf pan and bake at 325° for 1 hour. Great plain or with cream cheese.

IOWA SWEET ROLLS

Jacque Wallingford

1 pkg. yeast
1 c. warm water
1 egg

¼ cube margarine
5 c. flour
⅓ c. sugar

Dissolve yeast in ¼ c. warm water, with 1 T. sugar. Let rise in bowl. Combine margarine, flour, egg, water and sugar. Beat these ingredients together and add yeast. Kneed all ingredients and let rise for 1 hour. Kneed again and place in a large buttered bowl. Let rise again for 1 hour. Shape into roll shape and place in baking pan. Bake for 20 min. at 350. Spread the top of rolls with additional margarine the last 7 min. of baking time.

OLD FASHIONED PIE CRUST

Helen Holt

3 c. flour
½ tsp baking powder

1 c. margarine
ice cold water

Mix flour and baking powder. Mix in margarine with a fork and knife. Add water, a few tablespoons at a time, tossing gently until pea size balls form. Roll out on floured board. Makes 3 pie crusts.

SOUR CREAM COFFEE CAKE

Laurie Zamiska

¼ lb. butter
1 c. sugar
2 eggs
1 c. sour cream
1 tsp. baking soda
1½ c. flour

1½ tsp. baking powder
1 tsp. vanilla
TOPPING: ¼ c. sugar
2 T. chopped nuts (walnuts or
  almonds)
1 T. cinnamon

Cream butter and sugar. Add eggs, then sour cream which has been mixed with soda. Blend well. Add flour and baking powder. Blend in vanilla, Pour one half of mixture into greased, 9 inch square or tube pan. Sprinkle one half of topping over it. Pour the rest of the mixture and sprinkle with remaining topping. Bake at 350° for 45 minutes. Serve warm for tea or breakfast. (Topping can be made with brown sugar). "Some times called food of heaven".

SPICE MUFFINS

Judy Masterson

2 c. flour
1 c. sugar
1 tsp. soda, ground cloves,
  cinnamon and nutmeg
1 c. plus 2 T. buttermilk

1 egg
½ c. milted butter
½ c. chopped nuts and/ or
  raisins

Mix dry ingredients, then pour in butter, buttermilk and egg and mix well. Add nuts. Bake at 400° for 20 minutes.

VIRGINIA'S SWEET ROLLS

Virginia Manchester

½ c. warm water
2 tsp. salt
2 pkgs. dry yeast
2 eggs

1½ c. warm milk
½ c. shortening
½ c. sugar
7½ c. flour

Mix water and yeast until dissolved. Stir in next 5 ingredients and half of the flour. Stir with a spoon. Add enough flour so that it is easy to handle. Knead about 5 minutes until smooth and elastic. Round up in a greased bowl, cover and let rise in a warm place until doubled in bulk, about one hour. Punch down, let rise until double again. Divide into rolls. I always make crescents). Place rolls in pans and let rise in a warm place, about 15-20 minutes. Bake at 400° for 10- 20 minutes.

263841-14

Though our church has changed,
our faith remains the same.

Desserts

Helpful Hints

- Keep eggs at room temperature to create greater volume when whipping egg whites for meringue.

- Pie dough can be frozen. Roll dough out between sheets of plastic wrap, stack in a pizza box, and keep the box in the freezer. Defrost in the fridge and use as needed. Use within 2 months.

- Place your pie plate on a cake stand when ready to flute the edges of the pie. The cake stand will make it easier to turn the pie plate, and you won't have to stoop over.

- When making decorative pie edges, use a spoon for a scalloped edge. Use a fork to make crosshatched and herringbone patterns.

- When cutting butter into flour for pastry dough, the process is easier if you cut the butter into small pieces before adding it to the flour.

- Pumpkin and other custard-style pies are done when they jiggle slightly in the middle. Fruit pies are done when the pastry is golden, juices bubble, and fruit is tender.

- Keep the cake plate clean while frosting by sliding 6-inch strips of waxed paper under each side of the cake. Once the cake is frosted and the frosting is set, pull the strips away, leaving a clean plate.

- Create a quick decorating tube to ice your cake with chocolate. Put chocolate in a heat-safe, zipper-lock plastic bag. Immerse it in simmering water until the chocolate is melted. Snip off the tip of one corner, and squeeze the chocolate out of the bag.

- Achieve professionally decorated cakes with a silky, molten look by blow-drying the frosting with a hair dryer until the frosting melts slightly.

- To ensure that you have equal amounts of batter in each pan when making a layered cake, use a kitchen scale to measure the weight.

- Prevent cracking in your cheesecake by placing a shallow pan of hot water on the bottom oven rack and keeping the oven door shut during baking.

- A cheesecake needs several hours to chill and set.

- For a perfectly cut cheesecake, dip the knife into hot water and clean it after each cut. You can also hold a length of dental floss taut and pull it down through the cheesecake to make a clean cut across the diameter of the cake.

DESSERTS

BREAD PUDDING WITH BUTTER SAUCE

E J Sugar

Pudding: 1½ lb. loaf French bread
½ c, raisins
1 tsp. cinnamon
8 eggs
1 c. sugar
4 tsp. butter
Butter Sauce: ¾ c. butter
1½ c. sugar
2 T. cornstarch
1½ c. half and half
1½ tsp. vanilla

Into a well greased 9x13 pan, tear the bread into 1" chunks. Sprinkle with raisins and cinnamon. Toss a little to evenly distribute. Mix the eggs, sugar and milk and pour over the bread. Press down a little to get everything moistened. Dot the top with the butter and bake at 375° for 1 hour. Let cool 20 minutes before serving. Serve with warm butter sauce..In a heavy saucepan, mix the sugar and cornstarch, add the butter and gradually stir in the half and half. Cook and stir constantly until clear and thickened. Remove from the heat and add vanilla. (2 T. brandy can be added if desired).

CHOCOLATE PIE

Wanda Maurice

2 lg. wooden spoon Hersey chocolate
2 lg. wooden spoon corn starch
1¾ c. sugar
2 cans canned milk
5 egg yolks
5 egg whites for meringue

Mix together all ingredients in large pot and cook on low heat until the mixture comes to a boil and is thickened. Pour into a prepared and baked pie crust. Whip the egg whites and spread over the top of the chocolate mixture. Put this completed pie under the broiler until lightly browned and then put into the refrigerator.

CHOCOLATE PUDDING

Laurie Zamiska

½-¾ c. sugar
6 T. flour
¼ tsp.
3 c. milk
3 1 oz. sq. unsweetened chocolate squares, chopped
1 tsp. vanilla

Combine sugar, flour, salt in top of a double boiler, mixing well. Add milk gradually, stirring well. Add chocolate, then place over boiling water. Cook and stir until thickened. Continue cooking for 10 minutes, stirring occasionally. Remove from heat and add vanilla. Chill and serve.

CONGO BARS (BLONDE BROWNIES)

Mimi Ronaldson
Susie Freas

⅔ butter or margarine
2¼ c. brown sugar (1 lb. box)
2⅔ c. sifted flour
3 tsp. baking powder

½ tsp. salt
3 eggs
1 c. walnuts, chopped
1 6 oz. chocolate chips

Melt butter in a large saucepan. Stir in brown sugar. Remove from heat and let cool 10 minutes. Sift together flour, baking powder, and salt, then set aside. Beat eggs, one at a time into sugar mixture. Stir in flour mixture, then add nuts and chips. Mix well. Spread into 15" x 10" x 1" greased pan. Bake at 350° for 25 to 35 minutes.

DATE PUDDING CAKE

Jacque Wallingford

1 c. dates chopped
1 c. boiling water
1 tsp. (level) baking soda
1 T. butter
1 tsp. vanilla

1 egg
1¼ c. flour
1 c. sugar
½ c. walnuts or pecans

Add dates, soda, and butter to boiling water. Let cool about 1 hour. Add egg and vanilla, mix. Stir in flour and sugar. Adding nuts is optional. Bake 350° for 30-35 minutes in a 11 x 17 pan.

DUMP CAKE

Tony Waltman

2 cans of pie fruit (I make my own)
1½ boxes of white or french vanilla cake mix

2 sticks of butter (salted)

Dump fruit in to a 9 x 14 ungreased pan, and spread evenly. Dump dry cake mix into the pan, and spread evenly. Melt butter and pour on top evenly covering most of the dry mix. Bake at 350° for about 45 minutes or until golden brown. Can be served with whipped cream or ice cream. Tony's Aunt Marie made this crusty, buttery, and sweet cake. His favorite combination is apples with butter pecan cake mix.

FAVORITE LOUISVILLE PIE

Jeri Ross

1 9 inch pie shell, partially baked
½ c. flour
1 c. sugar
¼ t. salt

1 stick of butter, melted
2 T. bourbon
1 t. vanilla
1 c. chocolate chips
1 c. pecans, chopped

(continued)

Heat oven to 350°. Mix dry ingredients, then add the all the other ingredients. Pour this mixture into pie shell and bake until puffed and firm, 45- 50 minutes. To insure a crisp pie crust, bake for 8-9 minutes in 400° oven.

HAWAIIAN CAKE
Janet Hartenfeld

2 c. flour
2 c. sugar
2 tsp. baking soda
2 eggs
1 c. walnuts - chopped
1 20 oz. can crushed pineapple
   with juice

Topping:
1 8 oz. cream cheese
2 c. powdered sugar
1 cube melted butter
1 tsp. vanilla

Mix first six ingredients in large bowl and blend well. Pour mixture into greased and floured 9X13 pan. Bake for 40-45 minutes at 350°. To prepare the topping, mix all the four ingredients and beat well.. After the cake is baked and removed from the oven, poke holes in the cake and pour on the topping mixture. Broil cake with topping spread evenly, until brown.

LEMON ANGEL CAKE DESSERT
Judy Masterson

juice of 4 lemons
½ c. sugar
1 c. sweetened condensed milk

1 pt. heavy cream - whipped
1 angel food cake

Combine lemon juice, sugar and milk in bowl and mix together. Fold in whipped cream into mixture. Tear angel food cake into bite size pieces and place in 9 X 12 " pan. Pour mixture of lemon/whipped cream on top of the cake bits. Chill for 24 hours. Serves 12 people.

LEMON BARS
Virginia Manchester

2 c. flour
½ c. powdered sugar
1 c. melted butter
4 eggs

2 c. sugar
½ c. lemon juice
¼ c. flour
½ tsp. baking powdered

First layer: Mix all ingredients until mixture clings together. Press into 9 x 13 inch pan. Bake for 20 minutes at 350°. Second layer: Beat eggs, sugar, and juice. Sift flour and baking powder, adding to egg mixture. Pour over baked crust. Bake at 350° for 25 minutes. Sprinkle with powdered sugar. Cool, and cut into squares...

MANDARIN ORANGE CAKE
Wanda Maurice

**Cake: 1 pkg. Betty Crocker
yellow cake mix
½ c. oil
½ c. walnuts
4 eggs**

**11 oz can. mandarin oranges
Topping: 20 oz. can crushed
pineapple with juice
1- 4 oz. box vanilla pudding
1- 8 oz. Cool-Whip**

Grease and flour bottom of 9 x 13 pan. Mix cake mix, oil, walnuts, eggs, and mandarin orange. Bake at 350° for 35-40 minutes. Mix remaining ingredients together and spread over cake.

PUMPKIN BARS
Terri Joerg

**2 c. flour
2 tsp. baking powder
½ tsp. salt
2 tsp. cinnamon
4 eggs
2 c. pumpkin
1 tsp baking soda
2 c. sugar**

**1 c. oil
1 c. nuts
3 oz. pkg. cream cheese
6 T. butter
1 tsp. cream
1 tsp. vanilla
2 c. powdered sugar**

Mix first nine ingredients together and beat well. Put in greased and floured jelly roll pan. Bake at 350° for 30 minutes. Mix cream cheese, butter, cream, vanilla, and nuts together. Spread evenly over pumpkin cake. Cut and serve.

RHUBARB CRISP
Jacque Wallingford

**4 - 6 stalks of fresh rhubarb, cut
in pieces
¾ c. sugar
½ c. butter**

**1 c. quick cooking rolled oats
½ c. flour
½ c. brown sugar, firmly packed**

Combine rhubarb and sugar in bottom of 11 x 13 inch pan. Melt butter, stir in remaining ingredients. Spread this mixture over rhubarb. If you want more topping, just double the butter, rolled oats, flour and brown sugar. Bake in moderate oven (350) for 1 hour. Option: May substitute 2 cups cranberries and 3 cups unpeeled red apples that have been sliced.

RHUBARB BARS
E J Sugar

**Crust: ½ c. butter, room
temperature
5 tsp. powdered sugar
1 c, flour**

**Filling; 1 ½ c. sugar
¼ c. flour
2 c. rhubarb, finely chopped
2 eggs**

(continued)

Crust: Mix together and pat into a greased 9 inch pan. Bake at 350° for 10 minutes or until lightly colored around the edges. Filling: Mix in a bowl in order given, and set aside. When crust is baked, pour mixture over it and bake for 45 minutes. Before the bars are completely cooled, run a knife around the edges of the pan because it usually sticks around this area. Best served first day, because they are very moist and texture changes as they sit.

SOUR CREAM APPLE COFFEE CAKE

E J Sugar

2 granny smith apples, sliced	2 c. flour
¼ c. butter	1 tsp. baking powder
1 c. sugar	¼ tsp. salt
2 eggs	½ c. brown sugar
1 c. sour cream	1 T. cinnamon
½ tsp. vanilla	

Sauté sliced apples for 10 minutes on low heat. Add a little water if they seem dry. Set aside to cool. In a large bowl, cream the butter and sugar. Add the eggs, mixing well. Fold in the sour cream and vanilla. Sift in the flour, baking powder and salt together. Fold into the batter carefully to keep batter light. Mix brown sugar and cinnamon together in a small bowl. In a greased tube pan, spread ⅓ of batter, layer ½ apples over this and sprinkle with ½ sugar/cinnamon, repeat finishing with the last ⅓ batter. Bake at 350° for 1 hour. Cool, remove from pan. May glaze or dust top with powder confectionery sugar..

SUMAN (RICE CAKE)

Mila Pajel

3 c. sweet rice	1½ c. dark brown sugar
5 c. water	1 can plus ¼ c. coconut milk

Soak the 3 cups of sweet rice in 5 cups water for 1 hour. Steam cook rice (to only half cook) in the same soaking water. Mix 1 cup of dark brown sugar with the half-cooked rice, making sure there are no sugar lumps. Pour the can of coconut milk into the mixture of rice and sugar making sure the whole mixture is well blended. Then slow cook the mixture of sweet rice, sugar, milk for about 30 minutes or so until rice is of soft and almost dry consistency-fully cooked. This is now the suman part. In a separate small pot, bring to a simmer ½ c. dark brown sugar melted and well blended with ¼ cup of coconut milk into preferred consistency. This is the syrup to be used as glazing on top of the suman.

TEXAS CHOCOLATE CAKE

Fran Rudisill

Cake: 1 c, water
¼ c. cocoa
2 c. flour
2 c. sugar
½ c. buttermilk
2 eggs
1 tsp. baking soda

1 tsp. vanilla
Frosting: ½ c. butter
½ c. cocoa
6-7 T milk
1 16 oz box powdered sugar
1 tsp. vanilla
1 c. walnuts chopped

In saucepan: bring butter, cocoa, and water to boil, Set aside. Combine flour and sugar in large bowl. Add cocoa mixture to flour and sugar mixture. Add buttermilk, eggs, baking soda, and vanilla to cake mixture. Pour into jellyroll pan (11 x 7) and bake at 375° for 20-25 minutes. Make frosting while cake bakes. In same saucepan bring butter, cocoa, milk to a boil. Add powdered sugar and vanilla beating until smooth. Fold in nuts. Frost cake while still warm. Serves 24,

263841-14

Sunday School children love
the Brookside sculpture, Ocean Ballet.

Cookies
& Candy

Helpful Hints

- Unbaked cookie dough can be covered and refrigerated for up to 24 hours or frozen in an airtight container for up to 9 months.

- Bake one cookie sheet at a time on the middle oven rack.

- Decorate cookies with chocolate by placing cookies on a rack over waxed paper. Dip the tines of a fork into melted chocolate and wave the fork gently back and forth to make line decorations.

- Some cookies need indentations on top to fill with jam or chocolate. Use the rounded end of a honey dipper.

- Dip cookie cutters in flour or powdered sugar and shake off excess before cutting. For chocolate dough, dip cutters in baking cocoa.

- Tin coffee cans make excellent freezer containers for cookies.

- If you only have one cookie sheet on hand, line it with parchment paper. While one batch is baking, load a second sheet of parchment paper to have another batch ready to bake. Cleanup will be easier.

- When a recipe calls for packed brown sugar, fill the correct size measuring cup with sugar and use one cup size smaller to pack the brown sugar into its cup.

- Cut-up dried fruit often sticks to the blade of your knife. To prevent this problem, coat the blade of your knife with a thin film of vegetable spray before cutting.

- Instead of folding nuts into brownie batter, sprinkle on top of batter before baking. This keeps nuts crunchy instead of soggy.

- Only use glass or shiny metal pans. Dark or nonstick pans will cause brownies to become soggy and low in volume.

- When making bars, line pan with aluminum foil and prepare as directed. The bars can be lifted out, and cleanup is easy.

- Cutting bars is easier if you score the bars right as the pan leaves the oven. When the bars cool, cut along the scored lines.

- Use a double boiler for melting chocolate to prevent it from scorching. A slow cooker on the lowest setting also works well for melting chocolate, especially when coating a large amount of candy.

- Parchment paper provides an excellent nonstick surface for candy. Waxed paper should not be used for high-temperature candy.

CARAMEL CORN

Susie Freas

4 quarts popped corn
1 c. light brown sugar

1 stick margarine
⅓ c. white Karo syrup or honey

In a sauce pan bring sugar, margarine, and syrup to a boil stirring constantly, then let simmer 5 minutes without stirring. Place popped corn on a large greased baking pan..Pour syrup over popped corn using a wooden fork or spoon to stir and coat all corn. Place in 250° heated oven for 1 hour. Take out and turn corn to coat, every 15 minutes. Great for Halloween, or birthdays I have also added dried fruit and nuts before baking.

FORGOTTEN COOKIES
(Meringue)

Helen Holt

2 egg whites
pinch of salt
½ tsp. cream of tartar
¾ c. sugar

½ tsp. vanilla
1 c. chocolate bits
1 c. nuts

Preheat oven to 375° for 15 minutes. This is very important. Beat egg whites until frothy. Add salt and cream of tarter. While beating until stiff, add sugar 1 teaspoon at a time until glossy. Add vanilla. Fold in chocolate bits and nuts. Drop on buttered cookie sheet. Put in oven and TURN OFF HEAT. Let stand in oven overnite. Store tightly in covered tins.,

LEMON BARS

Susie Freas
Kathy Stephens

CRUST: 1 c. flour
½ c. butter
¼ c. powdered sugar
TOPPING: 2 eggs

1 c. granulated sugar
½ tsp baking powder
¼ tsp salt
2 T lemon juice

Cream first three ingredients. Pat into bottom of 8 x 8 pan. Bake 350° for 20 minutes. Stir together eggs, sugar, baking powder, salt, and lemon juice. Pour over baked bottom layer. Bake for about 25 minutes more. Top with confectionary sugar. Place sugar into a small strainer, use a spoon to dust sugar on to top. Cut into squares.

MICROWAVE PECAN/CASHEW BRITTLE

Pauline Krey

2 c. pecan haves or cashews	1 tsp. margarine
1 c. sugar	1 tsp. vanilla
½ c. white corn syrup	½ tsp. cinnamon
⅛ tsp. salt	1 tsp. baking soda

In greased 2 quart microwave bowl, cook sugar, corn syrup and salt on high for 2-3 minutes, until boiling. Stir mixture and cook for 4 more minutes. Add nuts, butter, vanilla and cinnamon. Cook for 2 more minutes. Immediately stir in baking soda until light and foamy. Quickly pour mixture on to greased cook sheet and spread evenly. Cool and break into pieces. Makes 1 pound.

MOLASSES COOKIES

Susie Freas

¾ c. shortening	2 c, flour.
1 c. sugar	½ tsp. ground cloves
¼ c. molasses	½ tsp. ginger
1 egg	1 tsp. cinnamon
2 tsp. baking soda	2 tsp. salt

Melt shortening in a 3 or 4 quart saucepan over low heat, let cool. Add sugar, molasses, and eggs. Beat well. Sift flour, baking soda, cloves, ginger, salt, and cinnamon. Add to first mixture. Mix well, then chill. Form 1" balls, then roll in granulated sugar. Place on greased cookie sheet, 2 inches apart. Bake at 375° for 8-10 minutes. My mother and Ii enjoyed making these cookies, when I was a child.

OATMEAL LACE COOKIES

Susie Freas

1 ½ c. sifted flour	1 c. sugar
1 tsp. baking soda	2 eggs
1 tsp. salt	1 tsp. vanilla
1 ½ c. butter (or 2 sticks	2 ½ c. oatmeal
margarine and ½ c. Crisco	1 ½ c. walnuts finely chopped
1 ½ c. brown sugar	

Preheat oven to 350° Sift together flour, baking soda, and salt. In large bowl beat butter with sugars until smooth and fluffy. Add eggs one at a time, beating well after each addition. Mix vanilla into batter. Gradually add sifted dry ingredients, mixing well. Add remaining ingredients. Drop by rounded teaspoons, 2 inches apart onto greased cookie sheet. Bake about 12 minutes, until golden brown. Remove from sheets while warm. Store in air tight container. Wax paper between layer helps these delicate cookies from breaking. A favorite family cookie.

PECAN, HAZELNUT, FILBERT BALLS

Regina Brown

1 c. sifted all-purpose flour
½ c. soft butter
1 c. finely chopped pecans or
  hazelnuts

2 T. granulated sugar
⅛ tsp. salt
1 tsp. vanilla
confectioner's sugar

In large bowl, combine all ingredients, except confectioner's sugar. With hands, mix until thoroughly blended. Refrigerate 30 minutes. Meanwhile, preheat oven to 375°. Using hands, roll dough into 1 ¼ inch balls. Place 1 inch apart on greased cookie sheets. Bake 15 to 20 minutes or until cookies are set but not brown. Let stand one minute before removing from cookie sheets. Remove to wire rack; cool slightly. Roll in confectioner's sugar while still warm, cool completely. Just before serving, roll in sugar once more. Makes about 20.

PERSIMMON COOKIES

Helen Macomber

½ c. butter, melted
2 c. sugar
2 eggs
2 c. persimmon pulp
4 c. flour

2 tsp. baking soda
1 tsp. nutmeg
1 tsp. cinnamon
2 c. raisins
2 c. nuts, chopped

Cream butter and sugar. Add eggs, then persimmon pulp. Combine with dry ingredients, then raisins and nuts. Bake at for minutes.

SPICY CHOCOLATE BARS

Pauline Krey

1 ½ c. shorting
1 ½ c. sugar
1 ½ c. brown sugar
4 eggs
2 tsp. vanilla
4 c. flour

2 tsp. soda
2 tsp. salt
3 tsp. cinnamon
1 tsp. ground cloves
1 tsp. nutmeg
4 c. chocolate chips

Cream both sugars and shortening, then add 1 egg at a time and beat well. Mix the rest of the ingredients together and add to the creamy mixture. Spread into ungreased 13 x 11 pan and bake at 350° for 40 minutes.

SUNSHINE CHOCOLATE CHIP COOKIES

E J Sugar

1 c. shortening
1 c. butter, room temperature
2 c. brown sugar
4 eggs
2 tsp. vanilla
5 c. flour

2 tsp. baking soda
2 c. quick-cook oatmeal
2 c. coconut
1 c. sunflower seeds
2 c. semi-sweet chocolate chips

Cream the sugars, butter, and shortening. Add the eggs and vanilla. Stir the soda into the flour and mix the rest of the batter. Stir in the remaining ingredients by hand. Bake on a greased cookie sheet at 350° for 10-12 minutes. The cookies will spread, so leave space. Makes 10 dozen.

WORLDS BEST COOKIES

Judy Masterson

1 c. butter
1 c. brown sugar
1 c. sugar
1 c. salad oil
1 egg
1 c. regular oatmeal

1 c. cornflakes, crushed
½ c. walnuts chopped
3½ c. flour
1 tsp. salt
1 tsp. vanilla

Cream together butter and both sugars, until light and fluffy. Add egg and salad oil to mixture and blend well. Blend in the oatmeal and cornflakes to the mixture. Then add flour, salt, walnuts and vanilla and mix well. Form the mixture into small balls (size to walnut) and place on greased cookie sheet. Flatten this ball with a fork. Bake these cookies at 325° oven for 12 minutes. After baking, cool the cookies on sheet for a few minutes before moving to plate or rack.

Ann Kientz, member and past
Historian for Women's Fellowship

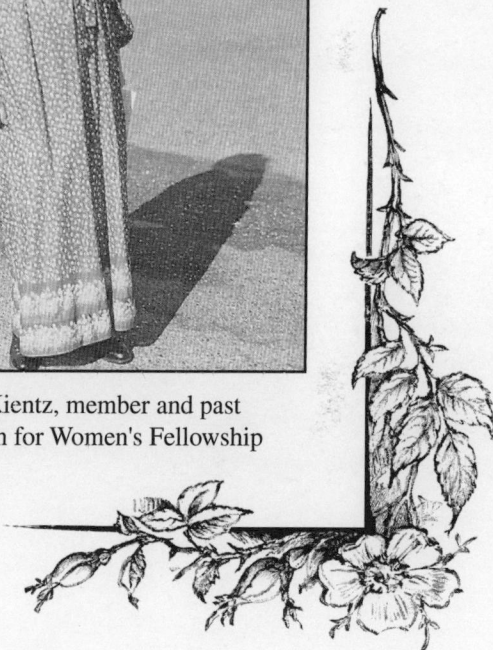

This & That

Helpful Hints

- Never overcook foods that are to be frozen. Foods will finish cooking when reheated. Don't refreeze cooked, thawed foods.

- When freezing foods, label each container with its contents and the date it was put into the freezer. Always use frozen, cooked foods within 1–2 months.

- To avoid teary eyes when cutting onions, cut them under cold running water or briefly place them in the freezer before cutting.

- Fresh lemon juice will remove onion scent from hands.

- To get the most juice out of fresh lemons, bring them to room temperature and roll them under your palm against the kitchen counter before cutting and squeezing.

- Add raw rice to the salt shaker to keep the salt free flowing.

- Transfer jelly and salad dressings to small plastic squeeze bottles – no more messy, sticky jars!

- Ice cubes will help sharpen garbage disposal blades.

- Separate stuck-together glasses by filling the inside glass with cold water and setting both in hot water.

- Clean CorningWare® by filling it with water and dropping in two denture cleaning tablets. Let stand for 30–45 minutes.

- Always spray your grill with nonstick cooking spray before grilling to avoid sticking.

- To make a simple polish for copper bottom cookware, mix equal parts of flour and salt with vinegar to create a paste.

- Purchase a new coffee grinder and mark it "spices." It can be used to grind most spices; however, cinnamon bark, nutmeg, and others must be broken up a little first. Clean the grinder after each use.

- In a large shaker, combine 6 parts salt and 1 part pepper for quick and easy seasoning.

- Save your store-bought bread bags and ties–they make perfect storage bags for homemade bread.

- Next time you need a quick ice pack, grab a bag of frozen peas or other vegetables out of the freezer.

THIS & THAT

APPLE BROWNIES
Jessie Evans

1 cube butter
1 c. sugar
1 egg
1 c. flour
½ tsp. baking soda
½ tsp. baking powder

½ tsp. salt
½ tsp. cinnamon
1 c. chopped apples
1 c. chopped walnuts
1 tsp. vanilla

Cream together butter and sugar and then add egg that is well beaten. Sift together flour, baking soda, baking powder, salt and cinnamon. Mix the creamed ingredients with the sifted ingredients. Add the apples, walnuts and vanilla to the mixture. Bake in 8 " square pan at 350° for 45-55 minutes.

APPLE CRISP
Mildred Ryckman
Alice Leatie Young

4 medium apples, peeled and
   diced
½ c. water
1 tsp cinnamon

½ c. butter
1 c. sugar
¾ c. flour

Place apples in greased baking dish and sprinkle with cinnamon. Mix in bowl, butter, sugar and flour until crumbly and spread over the apples. Bake uncovered at 350 for 90 minutes.

BAKED CHICKEN REUBEN
Cheryl Behrns

1 lg. jar sauerkraut, well drained
4 whole chicken breast-
   seasoned and halved

4 slices Swiss cheese
1¼ c. Thousand Island dressing
1 T. chopped parsley

In a buttered baking pan, placed chicken. Pour sauerkraut over the chicken and top with Swiss cheese slices. Pour the salad dressing over the cheese and cover the pan with foil. Bake at 325° for about 1 ½ hours and then remove foil and sprinkle with chopped parsley.

COCKTAIL NIBBLES

Marilyn Brown

6 oz. pkg. pretzels
1 pkg. Cheerios
1 pkg. Corn Chex
1 pkg. cheese puffs
1 can mixed nuts
1 Tb. garlic powder
1 Tb. onion powder
1 Tb. celery salt

¼ c. Worcestershire sauce
1 lb. salted peanuts
1 pkg. Rice Chex
1 pkg. Crispix
1 pkg. sesame sticks
1 cube butter
½ c. salad oil

Start oven at 225. Put cereals, nuts, puffs, pretzels and sesame sticks in large roasting pan. Mix melted butter, salad, oil, Worcestershire sauce and all spices over cereal mix. Bake for 1 ½ hours, stir occasionally.

COPPER PENNIES

Ruth Cunningham

2 lbs. carrots
1 medium onion, chopped
1 medium green pepper,
 chopped
1 can water chestnuts, sliced
1 can tomato soup

¾ c. white sugar
1 tsp. prepared mustard
1 tsp. Worcestershire sauce
½ c. wine vinegar
1 tsp. salt
½ c. oil

Slice carrots and cooked until crisp (5 minutes). Drain and cool. Mix the rest of the ingredients and pour over carrots to marinate for 12 to 24 hours. Serve as a vegetable and it keeps for a week in the refrigerator.

CRANBERRY SALAD

Cheryl Behrns

1 pkg lemon yellow
1 c. boiling water
½ c. pineapple, crushed and
 drained

1 c. whole cranberry sauce

Dissolve jello in boiling water. Add remaining ingredients. Refrigerate until firm.

CSIRKEPAPRIKAS - PAPRIKA CHICKEN

Bertha Green
Ron and Cyndy Green

1 onion - chopped
4 T. shortening
1 T. paprika
1 tsp. black pepper
2 T. salt
4 - 5 lbs. chicken pieces
1 ½ c. water

½ pt. sour cream
Gomboc (Dumplings)
3 eggs - well beaten
3 c. flour
3 T. sour cream
1 T. salt
½ c. water

Gomboc - Dumplings. Mix eggs, flour and sour cream together in bowl and beat well. Boil water and add salt. Drop a teaspoon of batter into boiling water and cook for about 10 minutes. Drain and rinse with cold water and place in large casserole dish. Csirkepaprikas - Paprika Chicken. Sauté chopped onion in shortening and add paprika, black pepper and salt and stir. Add chicken and cook for 10 minutes. Add water and cover and simmer until chicken is tender. Remove chicken. Add sour cream to pan and mix well. Arrange chicken on top of dumplings in the casserole dish and cover with sour cream mixture. Heat thoroughly.

FRENCH MINT PIE

Ruth Cunningham

1 c. powdered sugar
1 cube margarine
2 eggs
2 squares unsweetened chocolate
¼ tsp. mint flavoring

½ tsp. green food coloring
½ pint whipping cream and 2 T. sugar
1 precooked graham cracker crust

Cream margarine and add 1 egg at a time. Melt chocolate and add mint flavoring, then add to creamed mixture. Spread this into prepared pie crust. Whip whipping cream and green food coloring together and spread this on pie and freeze for 6 hours. Remove from freezer 30 minutes before serving.

FUDGE PUDDING

Mildred Ryckman
Alice Leatie Young

1 c. flour
2 t. baking powder
½ t. salt
¾ c. sugar
2 T. cocoa
½ c. milk

1 t. vanilla
2 T. melted shortening
¾ c. chopped walnuts
¾ c. brown sugar
4 T. cocoa
1 ¾ c. hot water

(continued)

263841-14

41

Sift together the first 5 ingredients. Mix the next 4 ingredients, milk, vanilla, melted shortening and walnuts and blend together with the sifted ingredients. Pour batter into a greased pan. Mix brown sugar and second cocoa and sprinkle over batter. Pour hot water over batter and bake at 350° for 40 minutes.

GLITTER TORTE

Jeannette W. Anderson
Jacque Wallingford

1½ c. fine graham cracker
  crumbs
⅓ c. sugar
½ c. butter, melted
1 pkg. orange flavored gelatin
1 pkg. lime favored gelatin
1 pkg. lemon flavored gelatin

¼ c. sugar
3 T. lemon juice
dash of salt
1 9 oz. can (1 cup) crushed
  pineapple
1½ c. heavy cream - whipped
¼ c. chopped walnuts

Combine the first three ingredients and press in bottom and sides of a 7 X 12 " pan. Set aside. In one bowl, dissolve orange gelatin with 1 cup hot water and then add 1 cup cold water and pour into 8 X 8" square pan and chill until firm. Then prepare the lime gelatin with the same process and chill until firm. After these two gelatins are firm, cut in ¼" cubes. Next, prepare lemon gelatin and sugar with 1 cup hot water and add pineapple, lemon juice, salt and ½ cup cold water. Chill until partially set and then whip until fluffy. Add the ¼' cubes of orange and lime gelatin to this mixture, saving a few of each cubes for top of pan. Whip the heavy cream and fold into mixture. Pour this mixture into crumb lined pan. Sprinkle the top of this pan with chopped walnuts and reserved gelatin cubes. Chill until set and then cut into wedges. Bright cubes of orange and green gelatin give this dish a look of "Jeweled Glitter".

HAM LOAF

Margaret Smith

¾ lb. ham
¾ lb. veal or beef
2 T. catsup
½ of green pepper, chopped
1 small onion, chopped

1 T. Worcestershire sauce
1 c. milk
salt & pepper
2 or 3 slices dark bread

Ground the first two meat ingredients. Mix the next five ingredients with the mixture of meat and place on the bread and place in a loaf pan. Put the loaf pan into a pan of water and bake for 1½ hours at 350.

HEARTLAND VEGETABLE BAKE

Ruth Cunningham

3 c. chopped red potatoes
2 T. water
1 16 oz. pkg. frozen broccoli, cauliflower and carrot medley
2 T. flour

3 T. butter
1 12 oz. can evaporated milk
2 vegetarian bouillon cubes
¼ c. seasoned bread crumbs

Microwave potatoes and water in covered dish for 8 minutes. Drain potatoes and return to casserole dish, then top with frozen vegetables. In pan, melt butter, add four and cook slowly until blended. Gradually stir in evaporated milk and bouillon cubes until sauce is slightly thickened. Pour this mixture over potato and vegetable in casserole dish and cover. Bake for 30 minutes at 350°. Uncover dish and sprinkle with bread crumbs and bake another 10 minutes.

KALACHES

Bertha Green
Ron and Cyndy Green

2 tsp. dry yeast
¼ c. warm water
½ c. buttermilk
3 c. flour
¼ c. butter, softened

½ c. sugar
2 eggs
1 tsp. salt
grated rind of lemon

Dissolve yeast in warm water. Add milk and 1 cup flour, mix gently and set aside to rise in a warm place. Cream butter and sugar and then add one egg at a time. Add salt, lemon rind and the rest of the flour to yeast mixture. Mix well and knead until elastic. Let this mixture rise in a warm place until double in size. Punch down and form into balls (size of a large walnut is good). Allow balls to rise and then use you fingers to create a crater in each ball for filling. Fillings can be stewed prunes or apricots or other fruit. Spoon fruit mixture into depressions in dough and sprinkle with poppy seeds. Bake in 375° oven until browned.

LAMB CURRY

Bertha Green
Ron and Cyndy Green

2 T. butter
2-3 T. chopped onion
1 T. flour
1 T. curry powder
1-2 T. ground cumin

2-3 chicken bouillon cubes
2-3 c. cooked lamb, cubed
1 pkg. frozen chopped spinach
1 T. lemon juice

Melt butter and lightly brown onion in butter. Stir in flour, curry powder and cumin. Cook for a few minutes and stirring constantly, so as to not allow mixture to brown. Stir in chicken bouillon and lemon juice and

(continued)

simmer; stirring until all is mixed. Add lamb and spinach and simmer over low heat for about half an hour. Serve over steamed rice.

LEMON PUDDING
Rebecca Freeman

2 T. butter
1 c. sugar
3 eggs (separated)

1 lg. lemon
3 T. flour
1½ c. milk

Cream butter and sugar until blended. Add egg yolk, flour and lemon juice to mixture. Next add milk and again mix well. In separate bowl, beat egg whites until they form peaks and fold into mixture. (Hint: bowl and beaters should be cold). Place the mixture into baking dish and then place the dish in shallow pan of water. Bake for 1 hour at 350°. Let cool before serving.

MEYER LEMON BREAD
Margaret Smith

1 c. shortening
2 c. sugar
3 c. flour
2 tsp. baking powder

1 tsp. salt
1 c. chopped walnuts
4 Meyer lemons
4 eggs

Cream together the shortening, sugar and juice of 4 lemons. Then add 1 egg at a time and blending the ingredients. In another bowl, shift flour, baking powder and salt. Blend the wet ingredients and milk with the dry ingredients. After these are fully blended, add walnuts and grated lemon peel from 2 of the lemons. Grease and flour wax paper lined loaf pan and bake at 350° for 1½ hours.

PERSIMMON COOKIES
Doris Haskell

1 c. persimmon pulp
1 c. walnut, chopped
1 c. raisins
1 c. brown sugar
½ c. shortening

1 t. soda
2 c. flour
1 egg
½ t. each cinnamon, ground
    cloves, nutmeg, & salt

Dissolve soda in persimmon pulp. Cream shortening and sugar and add in 1 egg. Add in part dry ingredients and persimmon mixture alternately. After this is complete add nuts and raisins. On ungreased cookie sheet, place small spoon full of cookie dough. Bake at 350° for 8 to 10 minutes.

263841-14

PETITE FOURS

Audrey Peterson

¼ c. butter
¼ c. shortening
1 c. sugar
½ tsp. vanilla
¼ tsp. almond extract
2 c. cake flour

3 tsp. baking powder
¼ tsp. salt
¾ c. milk
6 egg whites
¼ c. sugar

Cream butter and shortening thoroughly, and gradually add 1 cup sugar and continue to stir together. Then add vanilla and almond extract, stir until smooth. In another bowl, sift flour, baking powder and salt, 3 different times. Add small amount of creamed mixture and milk to the floured mixture and always mixing until smooth. Beat egg whites until foamy and gradually adding remaining ¼ cup of sugar and beat until forming peaks. Fold this into flour/creamy mixture. Pour this into a paper lined 13x11 pan and bake at 350° for 40 minutes. After the cake cools, cut in 2 x 2 inch squares and place them on wax paper covered cookie sheet and drip frosting over each little cake. Decorate cakes with candies or nuts and place in cupcake liners for serving.

PISTACHIO NUT PUDDING

Cheryl Behrns

1 18 oz. Cool Whip
1 6 oz. Pistachio Instant
  pudding mix
1 sm. can crushed pineapple
  with juice

1 pt. slim cottage cheese
2 small containers plain yogurt
½ c. chopped walnuts

Combine all ingredients, in large bowl and mix well. Refrigerate for 6 hours and serve.

RANCH STYLE BEANS

Jeannette W. Anderson
Jacque Wallingford

1 lb. ground beef
1 envelope green onion dip mix
2 16 oz. cans Pork and Beans in
  tomato sauce
1 16 oz. can kidney beans -
  drained

1 c. ketchup
2 T. prepared mustard
2 tsp. vinegar

Brown meat and then add all ingredients to Crock Pot and cook on low for 3 to 4 hours.

ROCKY ROAD FUDGE

Nora Imes

1 lg. pkg. chocolate chips
1 small pkg. butterscotch chips
1 c. crunchy peanut butter
3 c. miniature marshmallows
1 c. chopped nuts

Melt both chips, add peanut butter, marshmallows and nuts. Put into greased pan and cover with wax paper. Refrigerate for a few hours and cut into pieces.

SCALLOPED POTATOES

Cheryl Behrns

5 to 6 potatoes, pealed & sliced
1 can cream of mushroom soup
1 can evaporated milk
2 c. grated cheese
salt & pepper to taste
¾ stick of butter

Layer all ingredients (2 different layers) in large dish and frequently dot with butter. Cover and bake at 350°, until potatoes are tender (45 min.). Remove cover and cook for 15 min. until potatoes are lightly brown.

TACO SALAD

Ruth Cunningham

1 head of lettuce - cut into
    pieces
5 tomatoes - cut in small pieces
1 16 oz. can kidney beans,
    drained
1 onion, chopped
2 cans chopped black olives,
    drained
1 lb. ground beef
1 8 oz. can tomato sauce
1 pkg. taco seasoning mix
1 8 oz. bag of tortilla chips
1 8 oz. can of water

Brown ground beef and drain off fat. Add taco seasoning mix, tomato sauce and water. Bring to a boil, then reduce heat and simmer for about 20 minutes. In large salad bowl, combine all other ingredients and beef mixture. Toss with Russian or Catalina salad dressing. Serves 8 to 10 people.

TREASURE COOKIES

Frances Fagler

1 ½ c. crushed graham crackers
½ c. flour
2 tsp. baking powder
1 can Eagle Brand milk
½ c. margarine
½ c. raisins or chocolate chips
1 ½ c. shredded coconut
1 c. chopped walnuts

Blend the first 5 ingredients, mixing well. Add the rest of the ingredients. On greased cookie sheet, drop large teaspoon size amounts. Bake at 375° for 8 - 10 minutes.

263841-14

VENUS DEMILO SOUP

Marilyn Brown

1 lb. ground beef
1 lg. onion, diced
1 can - 28 oz. tomatoes, cut-up
1 can-28 oz. water
1 lg. pkg. frozen mixed
  vegetables
5 cubes beef bouillon

1 pkg. onion soup mix
1 T. sugar
1 tsp. oregano
1 tsp. basil
¾ c. orzo
Parmesan cheese

Brown meat with onion and drain off fat. Add all the other ingredients, except orzo. Simmer for 15 minutes. Add orzo and again simmer for another 15 minutes. Serve with Parmesan cheese. Serves 12 people.

WALNUT CHERRY SQUARES

Bertha Green
Ron and Cyndy Green

1 cube butter
1½ c, sugar
6 egg yolks
1 tsp. vanilla
½ pint sour cream

16 maraschino cherries - diced
1 lb. walnuts, ground
1½ c. cake flour - sifted
1 tsp. baking soda
6 egg whites, beaten

Beat butter, sugar, egg yolks, sour cream and vanilla. Add flour and baking soda and mix together. Add cherries and walnuts and fold in beaten egg whites. Pour into a 7 X 15 square pan or 2 12 inch round pans. Bake at 350° for 30 -35 minutes.

WALNUT SQUARES

Cheryl Behrns

1 tsp.
½ c. butter
dash of salt
1½ c. brown sugar
2 eggs

3 T. flour
dash of salt
1 c. chopped walnuts
½ c. shredded coconut
1 tsp. vanilla

Combine the first three ingredients in a bowl. Spread this in a 8 inch square pan and press this with the back of a spoon. Bake for five minutes at 350°. In another bowl mix the rest of the ingredients and spread on top of the baked crust in the 8 inch square pan. Bake this for 20 minutes at 350°.

Recipe Favorites

263841-14

INDEX OF CONTRIBUTORS

263841-14

INDEX OF RECIPES

263841-14

PANTRY BASICS

A WELL-STOCKED PANTRY provides all the makings for a good meal. With the right ingredients, you can quickly create a variety of satisfying, delicious meals for family or guests. Keeping these items in stock also means avoiding extra trips to the grocery store, saving you time and money. Although everyone's pantry is different, there are basic items you should always have. Add other items according to your family's needs. For example, while some families consider chips, cereals and snacks as must-haves, others can't be without feta cheese and imported olives. Use these basic pantry suggestions as a handy reference list when creating your grocery list. Don't forget refrigerated items like milk, eggs, cheese and butter.

STAPLES

Baker's chocolate
Baking powder
Baking soda
Barbeque sauce
Bread crumbs (plain or seasoned)
Chocolate chips
Cocoa powder
Cornmeal
Cornstarch
Crackers
Flour
Honey
Ketchup
Lemon juice
Mayonnaise or salad dressing
Non-stick cooking spray
Nuts (almonds, pecans, walnuts)
Oatmeal
Oil (olive, vegetable)
Pancake baking mix
Pancake syrup
Peanut butter
Shortening
Sugar (granulated, brown, powdered)
Vinegar

PACKAGED/CANNED FOODS

Beans (canned, dry)
Broth (beef, chicken)
Cake mixes with frosting
Canned diced tomatoes
Canned fruit
Canned mushrooms
Canned soup
Canned tomato paste & sauce
Canned tuna & chicken
Cereal
Dried soup mix
Gelatin (flavored or plain)
Gravies
Jarred Salsa
Milk (evaporated, sweetened condensed)
Non-fat dry milk
Pastas
Rice (brown, white)
Spaghetti sauce

SPICES/SEASONINGS

Basil
Bay leaves
Black pepper
Bouillon cubes (beef, chicken)
Chives
Chili powder
Cinnamon
Mustard (dried, prepared)
Garlic powder or salt
Ginger
Nutmeg
Onion powder or salt
Oregano
Paprika
Parsley
Rosemary
Sage
Salt
Soy sauce
Tarragon
Thyme
Vanilla
Worcestershire sauce
Yeast

HERBS & SPICES

DRIED VS. FRESH. While dried herbs are convenient, they don't generally have the same purity of flavor as fresh herbs. Ensure dried herbs are still fresh by checking if they are green and not faded. Crush a few leaves to see if the aroma is still strong. Always store them in an air-tight container away from light and heat.

BASIL — Sweet, warm flavor with an aromatic odor. Use whole or ground. Good with lamb, fish, roast, stews, beef, vegetables, dressing and omelets.

BAY LEAVES — Pungent flavor. Use whole leaf but remove before serving. Good in vegetable dishes, seafood, stews and pickles.

CARAWAY — Spicy taste and aromatic smell. Use in cakes, breads, soups, cheese and sauerkraut.

CELERY SEED — Strong taste which resembles the vegetable. Can be used sparingly in pickles and chutney, meat and fish dishes, salads, bread, marinades, dressings and dips.

CHIVES — Sweet, mild flavor like that of onion. Excellent in salads, fish, soups and potatoes.

CILANTRO — Use fresh. Excellent in salads, fish, chicken, rice, beans and Mexican dishes.

CINNAMON — Sweet, pungent flavor. Widely used in many sweet baked goods, chocolate dishes, cheesecakes, pickles, chutneys and hot drinks.

CORIANDER — Mild, sweet, orangy flavor and available whole or ground. Common in curry powders and pickling spice and also used in chutney, meat dishes, casseroles, Greek-style dishes, apple pies and baked goods.

CURRY POWDER — Spices are combined to proper proportions to give a distinct flavor to meat, poultry, fish and vegetables.

DILL — Both seeds and leaves are flavorful. Leaves may be used as a garnish or cooked with fish, soup, dressings, potatoes and beans. Leaves or the whole plant may be used to flavor pickles.

FENNEL — Sweet, hot flavor. Both seeds and leaves are used. Use in small quantities in pies and baked goods. Leaves can be boiled with fish.

DILL
Seeds

HERBS *&* SPICES

GINGER
A pungent root, this aromatic spice is sold fresh, dried or ground. Use in pickles, preserves, cakes, cookies, soups and meat dishes.

MARJORAM
May be used both dried or green. Use to flavor fish, poultry, omelets, lamb, stew, stuffing and tomato juice.

MINT
Aromatic with a cool flavor. Excellent in beverages, fish, lamb, cheese, soup, peas, carrots and fruit desserts.

NUTMEG
Whole or ground. Used in chicken and cream soups, cheese dishes, fish cakes, and with chicken and veal. Excellent in custards, milk puddings, pies and cakes.

OREGANO
Strong, aromatic odor. Use whole or ground in tomato juice, fish, eggs, pizza, omelets, chili, stew, gravy, poultry and vegetables.

PAPRIKA
A bright red pepper, this spice is used in meat, vegetables and soups or as a garnish for potatoes, salads or eggs.

PARSLEY
Best when used fresh, but can be used dried as a garnish or as a seasoning. Try in fish, omelets, soup, meat, stuffing and mixed greens.

ROSEMARY
Very aromatic. Can be used fresh or dried. Season fish, stuffing, beef, lamb, poultry, onions, eggs, bread and potatoes. Great in dressings.

SAFFRON
Aromatic, slightly bitter taste. Only a pinch needed to flavor and color dishes such as bouillabaisse, chicken soup, rice, paella, fish sauces, buns and cakes. Very expensive, so where a touch of color is needed, use turmeric instead, but the flavor will not be the same.

SAGE
Use fresh or dried. The flowers are sometimes used in salads. May be used in tomato juice, fish, omelets, beef, poultry, stuffing, cheese spreads and breads.

TARRAGON
Leaves have a pungent, hot taste. Use to flavor sauces, salads, fish, poultry, tomatoes, eggs, green beans, carrots and dressings.

THYME
Sprinkle leaves on fish or poultry before broiling or baking. Throw a few sprigs directly on coals shortly before meat is finished grilling.

TURMERIC
Aromatic, slightly bitter flavor. Should be used sparingly in curry powder and relishes and to color cakes and rice dishes.

Use 3 times more fresh herbs if substituting fresh for dried.

BAKING BREADS

HINTS FOR BAKING BREADS

- Kneading dough for 30 seconds after mixing improves the texture of baking powder biscuits.

- Instead of shortening, use cooking or salad oil in waffles and hot cakes.

- When bread is baking, a small dish of water in the oven will help keep the crust from hardening.

- Dip a spoon in hot water to measure shortening, butter, etc., and the fat will slip out more easily.

- Small amounts of leftover corn may be added to pancake batter for variety.

- To make bread crumbs, use the fine cutter of a food grinder and tie a large paper bag over the spout in order to prevent flying crumbs.

- When you are doing any sort of baking, you get better results if you remember to preheat your cookie sheet, muffin tins or cake pans.

3 RULES FOR USE OF LEAVENING AGENTS

1. In simple flour mixtures, use 2 teaspoons baking powder to leaven 1 cup flour. Reduce this amount $1/2$ teaspoon for each egg used.

2. To 1 teaspoon soda, use 2 $1/4$ teaspoons cream of tartar, 2 cups freshly soured milk or 1 cup molasses.

3. To substitute soda and an acid for baking powder, divide the amount of baking powder by 4. Take that as your measure and add acid according to rule 2.

PROPORTIONS OF BAKING POWDER TO FLOUR

biscuits ....to 1 cup flour use 1 $1/4$ tsp. baking powder
cake with oil ....to 1 cup flour use 1 tsp. baking powder
muffins ....to 1 cup flour use 1 $1/2$ tsp. baking powder
popovers ....to 1 cup flour use 1 $1/4$ tsp. baking powder
waffles ....to 1 cup flour use 1 $1/4$ tsp. baking powder

PROPORTIONS OF LIQUID TO FLOUR

pour batter ....to 1 cup liquid use 1 cup flour
drop batter ....to 1 cup liquid use 2 to 2 $1/2$ cups flour
soft dough ....to 1 cup liquid use 3 to 3 $1/2$ cups flour
stiff dough ....to 1 cup liquid use 4 cups flour

TIME & TEMPERATURE CHART

Breads	Minutes	Temperature
biscuits	12 - 15	400° - 450°
cornbread	25 - 30	400° - 425°
gingerbread	40 - 50	350° - 370°
loaf	50 - 60	350° - 400°
nut bread	50 - 75	350°
popovers	30 - 40	425° - 450°
rolls	20 - 30	400° - 450°

BAKING DESSERTS

PERFECT COOKIES

Cookie dough that must be rolled is much easier to handle after it has been refrigerated for 10 to 30 minutes. This keeps the dough from sticking, even though it may be soft. If not done, the soft dough may require more flour and too much flour makes cookies hard and brittle. Place on a floured board only as much dough as can be easily managed. Flour the rolling pin slightly and roll lightly to desired thickness. Cut shapes close together and add trimmings to dough that needs to be rolled. Place pans or sheets in upper third of oven. Watch cookies carefully while baking in order to avoid burned edges. When sprinkling sugar on cookies, try putting it into a salt shaker in order to save time.

PERFECT PIES

• Pie crust will be better and easier to make if all the ingredients are cool.

• The lower crust should be placed in the pan so that it covers the surface smoothly. Air pockets beneath the surface will push the crust out of shape while baking.

• Folding the top crust over the lower crust before crimping will keep juices in the pie.

• When making custard pie, bake at a high temperature for about 10 minutes to prevent a soggy crust. Then finish baking at a low temperature.

• When making cream pie, sprinkle crust with powdered sugar in order to prevent it from becoming soggy.

PERFECT CAKES

• Fill cake pans two-thirds full and spread batter into corners and sides, leaving a slight hollow in the center.

• Cake is done when it shrinks from the sides of the pan or if it springs back when touched lightly with the finger.

• After removing a cake from the oven, place it on a rack for about 5 minutes. Then, the sides should be loosened and the cake turned out on a rack in order to finish cooling.

• Do not frost cakes until thoroughly cool.

• Icing will remain where you put it if you sprinkle cake with powdered sugar first.

TIME & TEMPERATURE CHART

Dessert	Time	Temperature
butter cake, layer	20 - 40 min.	380° - 400°
butter cake, loaf	40 - 60 min.	360° - 400°
cake, angel	50 - 60 min.	300° - 360°
cake, fruit	3 - 4 hrs.	275° - 325°
cake, sponge	40 - 60 min.	300° - 350°
cookies, molasses	18 - 20 min.	350° - 375°
cookies, thin	10 - 12 min.	380° - 390°
cream puffs	45 - 60 min.	300° - 350°
meringue	40 - 60 min.	250° - 300°
pie crust	20 - 40 min.	400° - 500°

VEGETABLES & FRUITS

COOKING TIME TABLE

Vegetable	Cooking Method	Time
artichokes	boiled	40 min.
	steamed	45 - 60 min.
asparagus tips	boiled	10 - 15 min.
beans, lima	boiled	20 - 40 min.
	steamed	60 min.
beans, string	boiled	15 - 35 min.
	steamed	60 min.
beets, old	boiled or steamed	1 - 2 hours.
beets, young with skin	boiled	30 min.
	steamed	60 min.
	baked	70 - 90 min.
broccoli, flowerets	boiled	5 - 10 min.
broccoli, stems	boiled	20 - 30 min.
brussels sprouts	boiled	20 - 30 min.
cabbage, chopped	boiled	10 - 20 min.
	steamed	25 min.
carrots, cut across	boiled	8 - 10 min.
	steamed	40 min.
cauliflower, flowerets	boiled	8 - 10 min.
cauliflower, stem down	boiled	20 - 30 min.
corn, green, tender	boiled	5 - 10 min.
	steamed	15 min.
	baked	20 min.
corn on the cob	boiled	8 - 10 min.
	steamed	15 min.
eggplant, whole	boiled	30 min.
	steamed	40 min.
	baked	45 min.
parsnips	boiled	25 - 40 min.
	steamed	60 min.
	baked	60 - 75 min.
peas, green	boiled or steamed	5 - 15 min.
potatoes	boiled	20 - 40 min.
	steamed	60 min.
	baked	45 - 60 min.
pumpkin or squash	boiled	20 - 40 min.
	steamed	45 min.
	baked	60 min.
tomatoes	boiled	5 - 15 min.
turnips	boiled	25 - 40 min.

DRYING TIME TABLE

Fruit	Sugar or Honey	Cooking Time
apricots	1/4 c. for each cup of fruit	about 40 min.
figs	1 T. for each cup of fruit	about 30 min.
peaches	1/4 c. for each cup of fruit	about 45 min.
prunes	2 T. for each cup of fruit	about 45 min.

VEGETABLES & FRUITS

BUYING FRESH VEGETABLES

Artichokes: Look for compact, tightly closed heads with green, clean-looking leaves. Avoid those with leaves that are brown or separated.

Asparagus: Stalks should be tender and firm; tips should be close and compact. Choose the stalks with very little white; they are more tender. Use asparagus soon because it toughens quickly.

Beans, Snap: Those with small seeds inside the pods are best. Avoid beans with dry-looking pods.

Broccoli, Brussels Sprouts and Cauliflower: Flower clusters on broccoli and cauliflower should be tight and close together. Brussels sprouts should be firm and compact. Smudgy, dirty spots may indicate pests or disease.

Cabbage and Head Lettuce: Choose heads that are heavy for their size. Avoid cabbage with worm holes and lettuce with discoloration or soft rot.

Cucumbers: Choose long, slender cucumbers for best quality. May be dark or medium green, but yellow ones are undesirable.

Mushrooms: Caps should be closed around the stems. Avoid black or brown gills.

Peas and Lima Beans: Select pods that are well-filled but not bulging. Avoid dried, spotted, yellow or limp pods.

BUYING FRESH FRUITS

Bananas: Skin should be free of bruises and black or brown spots. Purchase them slightly green and allow them to ripen at room temperature.

Berries: Select plump, solid berries with good color. Avoid stained containers which indicate wet or leaky berries. Berries with clinging caps, such as blackberries and raspberries, may be unripe. Strawberries without caps may be overripe.

Melons: In cantaloupes, thick, close netting on the rind indicates best quality. Cantaloupes are ripe when the stem scar is smooth and the space between the netting is yellow or yellow-green. They are best when fully ripe with fruity odor.

Honeydews are ripe when rind has creamy to yellowish color and velvety texture. Immature honeydews are whitish-green.

Ripe watermelons have some yellow color on one side. If melons are white or pale green on one side, they are not ripe.

Oranges, Grapefruit and Lemons: Choose those heavy for their size. Smoother, thinner skins usually indicate more juice. Most skin markings do not affect quality. Oranges with a slight greenish tinge may be just as ripe as fully colored ones. Light or greenish-yellow lemons are more tart than deep yellow ones. Avoid citrus fruits showing withered, sunken or soft areas.

NAPKIN FOLDING

FOR BEST RESULTS, use well-starched linen napkins if possible. For more complicated folds, 24-inch napkins work best. Practice the folds with newspapers. Children will have fun decorating the table once they learn these attractive folds!

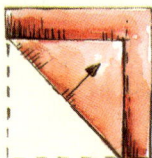

1, 2

3

4

SHIELD

Easy fold. Elegant with monogram in corner.

Instructions:
1. Fold into quarter size. If monogrammed, ornate corner should face down.
2. Turn up folded corner three-quarters.
3. Overlap right side and left side points.
4. Turn over; adjust sides so they are even, single point in center.
5. Place point up or down on plate, or left of plate.

ROSETTE

Elegant on plate.

Instructions:
1. Fold left and right edges to center, leaving 1/2" opening along center.
2. Pleat firmly from top edge to bottom edge. Sharpen edges with hot iron.
3. Pinch center together. If necessary, use small piece of pipe cleaner to secure and top with single flower.
4. Spread out rosette.

1

2

3

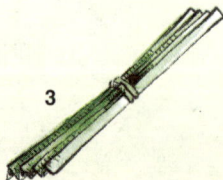

4

NAPKIN FOLDING

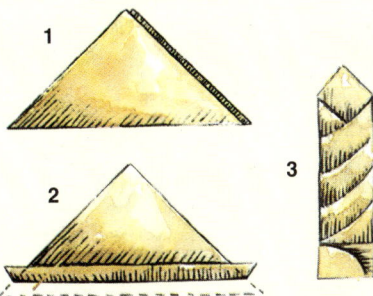

CANDLE

Easy to do; can be decorated.

Instructions:
1. Fold into triangle, point at top.
2. Turn lower edge up 1".
3. Turn over, folded edge down.
4. Roll tightly from left to right.
5. Tuck in corner. Stand upright.

FAN

Pretty in napkin ring or on plate.

Instructions:
1. Fold top and bottom edges to center.
2. Fold top and bottom edges to center a second time.
3. Pleat firmly from the left edge. Sharpen edges with hot iron.
4. Spread out fan. Balance flat folds of each side on table. Well-starched napkins will hold shape.

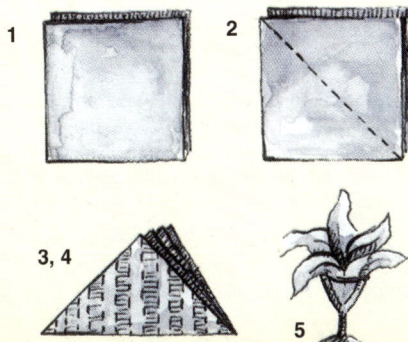

LILY

Effective and pretty on table.

Instructions:
1. Fold napkin into quarters.
2. Fold into triangle, closed corner to open points.
3. Turn two points over to other side. (Two points are on either side of closed point.)
4. Pleat.
5. Place closed end in glass. Pull down two points on each side and shape.

MEASUREMENTS & SUBSTITUTIONS

MEASUREMENTS

a pinch	1/8 teaspoon or less
3 teaspoons	1 tablespoon
4 tablespoons	1/4 cup
8 tablespoons	1/2 cup
12 tablespoons	3/4 cup
16 tablespoons	1 cup
2 cups	1 pint
4 cups	1 quart
4 quarts	1 gallon
8 quarts	1 peck
4 pecks	1 bushel
16 ounces	1 pound
32 ounces	1 quart
1 ounce liquid	2 tablespoons
8 ounces liquid	1 cup

Use standard measuring spoons and cups. All measurements are level.

C° TO F° CONVERSION

120° C	250° F
140° C	275° F
150° C	300° F
160° C	325° F
180° C	350° F
190° C	375° F
200° C	400° F
220° C	425° F
230° C	450° F

Temperature conversions are estimates.

SUBSTITUTIONS

Ingredient	Quantity	Substitute
baking powder	1 teaspoon	1/4 tsp. baking soda plus 1/2 tsp. cream of tartar
chocolate	1 square (1 oz.)	3 or 4 T. cocoa plus 1 T. butter
cornstarch	1 tablespoon	2 T. flour or 2 tsp. quick-cooking tapioca
cracker crumbs	3/4 cup	1 c. bread crumbs
dates	1 lb.	1 1/2 c. dates, pitted and cut
dry mustard	1 teaspoon	1 T. prepared mustard
flour, self-rising	1 cup	1 c. all-purpose flour, 1/2 tsp. salt, and 1 tsp. baking powder
herbs, fresh	1 tablespoon	1 tsp. dried herbs
ketchup or chili sauce	1 cup	1 c. tomato sauce plus 1/2 c. sugar and 2 T. vinegar (for use in cooking)
milk, sour	1 cup	1 T. lemon juice or vinegar plus sweet milk to make 1 c. (let stand 5 minutes)
whole	1 cup	1/2 c. evaporated milk plus 1/2 c. water
min. marshmallows	10	1 lg. marshmallow
onion, fresh	1 small	1 T. instant minced onion, rehydrated
sugar, brown	1/2 cup	2 T. molasses in 1/2 c. granulated sugar
powdered	1 cup	1 c. granulated sugar plus 1 tsp. cornstarch
tomato juice	1 cup	1/2 c. tomato sauce plus 1/2 c. water

When substituting cocoa for chocolate in cakes, the amount of flour must be reduced. Brown and white sugars usually can be interchanged.

SUGAR

EQUIVALENCY CHART

Food	Quantity	Yield
apple	1 medium	1 cup
banana, mashed	1 medium	1/3 cup
bread	1 1/2 slices	1 cup soft crumbs
bread	1 slice	1/4 cup fine, dry crumbs
butter	1 stick or 1/4 pound	1/2 cup
cheese, American, cubed	1 pound	2 2/3 cups
American, grated	1 pound	5 cups
cream cheese	3-ounce package	6 2/3 tablespoons
chocolate, bitter	1 square	1 ounce
cocoa	1 pound	4 cups
coconut	1 1/2 pound package	2 2/3 cups
coffee, ground	1 pound	5 cups
cornmeal	1 pound	3 cups
cornstarch	1 pound	3 cups
crackers, graham	14 squares	1 cup fine crumbs
saltine	28 crackers	1 cup fine crumbs
egg	4 - 5 whole	1 cup
whites	8 - 10	1 cup
yolks	10 - 12	1 cup
evaporated milk	1 cup	3 cups whipped
flour, cake, sifted	1 pound	4 1/2 cups
rye	1 pound	5 cups
white, sifted	1 pound	4 cups
white, unsifted	1 pound	3 3/4 cups
gelatin, flavored	3 1/4 ounces	1/2 cup
unflavored	1/4 ounce	1 tablespoon
lemon	1 medium	3 tablespoon juice
marshmallows	16	1/4 pound
noodles, cooked	8-ounce package	7 cups
uncooked	4 ounces (1 1/2 cups)	2 - 3 cups cooked
macaroni, cooked	8-ounce package	6 cups
macaroni, uncooked	4 ounces (1 1/4 cups)	2 1/4 cups cooked
spaghetti, uncooked	7 ounces	4 cups cooked
nuts, chopped	1/4 pound	1 cup
almonds	1 pound	3 1/2 cups
walnuts, broken	1 pound	3 cups
walnuts, unshelled	1 pound	1 1/2 to 1 3/4 cups
onion	1 medium	1/2 cup
orange	3 - 4 medium	1 cup juice
raisins	1 pound	3 1/2 cups
rice, brown	1 cup	4 cups cooked
converted	1 cup	3 1/2 cups cooked
regular	1 cup	3 cups cooked
wild	1 cup	4 cups cooked
sugar, brown	1 pound	2 1/2 cups
powdered	1 pound	3 1/2 cups
white	1 pound	2 cups
vanilla wafers	22	1 cup fine crumbs
zwieback, crumbled	4	1 cup

FOOD QUANTITIES

FOR LARGE SERVINGS

	25 Servings	50 Servings	100 Servings
Beverages:			
coffee	½ pound & 1 ½ gallons water	1 pound & 3 gallons water	2 pounds & 6 gallons water
lemonade	10 - 15 lemons & 1 ½ gallons water	20 - 30 lemons & 3 gallons water	40 - 60 lemons & 6 gallons water
tea	1/12 pound & 1 ½ gallons water	1/6 pound & 3 gallons water	1/3 pound & 6 gallons water
Desserts:			
layered cake	1 12" cake	3 10" cakes	6 10" cakes
sheet cake	1 10" x 12" cake	1 12" x 20" cake	2 12" x 20" cakes
watermelon	37 ½ pounds	75 pounds	150 pounds
whipping cream	¾ pint	1 ½ to 2 pints	3 - 4 pints
Ice cream:			
brick	3 ¼ quarts	6 ½ quarts	13 quarts
bulk	2 ¼ quarts	4 ½ quarts or 1 ¼ gallons	9 quarts or 2 ½ gallons
Meat, poultry or fish:			
fish	13 pounds	25 pounds	50 pounds
fish, fillets or steak	7 ½ pounds	15 pounds	30 pounds
hamburger	9 pounds	18 pounds	35 pounds
turkey or chicken	13 pounds	25 - 35 pounds	50 - 75 pounds
wieners (beef)	6 ½ pounds	13 pounds	25 pounds
Salads, casseroles:			
baked beans	¾ gallon	1 ¼ gallons	2 ½ gallons
jello salad	¾ gallon	1 ¼ gallons	2 ½ gallons
potato salad	4 ¼ quarts	2 ¼ gallons	4 ½ gallons
scalloped potatoes	4 ½ quarts or 1 12" x 20" pan	9 quarts or 2 ¼ gallons	18 quarts 4 ½ gallons
spaghetti	1 ¼ gallons	2 ½ gallons	5 gallons
Sandwiches:			
bread	50 slices or 3 1-lb. loaves	100 slices or 6 1-lb. loaves	200 slices or 12 1-lb. loaves
butter	½ pound	1 pound	2 pounds
lettuce	1 ½ heads	3 heads	6 heads
mayonnaise	1 cup	2 cups	4 cups
mixed filling			
meat, eggs, fish	1 ½ quarts	3 quarts	6 quarts
jam, jelly	1 quart	2 quarts	4 quarts

QUICK FIXES

PRACTICALLY EVERYONE has experienced that dreadful moment in the kitchen when a recipe failed and dinner guests have arrived. Perhaps a failed timer, distraction or a missing or mismeasured ingredient is to blame. These handy tips can save the day!

Acidic foods – Sometimes a tomato-based sauce will become too acidic. Add baking soda, one teaspoon at a time, to the sauce. Use sugar as a sweeter alternative.

Burnt food on pots and pans – Allow the pan to cool on its own. Remove as much of the food as possible. Fill with hot water and add a capful of liquid fabric softener to the pot; let it stand for a few hours. You'll have an easier time removing the burnt food.

Chocolate seizes – Chocolate can seize (turn coarse and grainy) when it comes into contact with water. Place seized chocolate in a metal bowl over a large saucepan with an inch of simmering water in it. Over medium heat, slowly whisk in warm heavy cream. Use 1/4 cup cream to 4 ounces of chocolate. The chocolate will melt and become smooth.

Forgot to thaw whipped topping – Thaw in microwave for 1 minute on the defrost setting. Stir to blend well. Do not over thaw!

Hands smell like garlic or onion – Rinse hands under cold water while rubbing them with a large stainless steel spoon.

Hard brown sugar – Place in a paper bag and microwave for a few seconds, or place hard chunks in a food processor.

Jell-O too hard – Heat on a low microwave power setting for a very short time.

Lumpy gravy or sauce – Use a blender, food processor or simply strain.

No tomato juice – Mix 1/2 cup ketchup with 1/2 cup water.

Out of honey – Substitute 1 1/4 cups sugar dissolved in 1 cup water.

Overcooked sweet potatoes or carrots – Softened sweet potatoes and carrots make a wonderful soufflé with the addition of eggs and sugar. Consult your favorite cookbook for a good soufflé recipe. Overcooked sweet potatoes can also be used as pie filling.

Sandwich bread is stale – Toast or microwave bread briefly. Otherwise, turn it into bread crumbs. Bread exposed to light and heat will hasten its demise, so consider using a bread box. If the bread will not be eaten within a few days, store half in the freezer.

Soup, sauce, gravy too thin – Add 1 tablespoon of flour to hot soup, sauce or gravy. Whisk well (to avoid lumps) while the mixture is boiling. Repeat if necessary.

Sticky rice – Rinse rice with warm water.

Stew or soup is greasy – Refrigerate and remove grease once it congeals. Another trick is to lay cold lettuce leaves over the hot stew for about 10 seconds and then remove. Repeat as necessary.

Too salty – Add a little sugar and vinegar. For soups or sauces, add a raw peeled potato.

Too sweet – Add a little vinegar or lemon juice.

Undercooked cakes and cookies – Serve over vanilla ice cream. You can also layer pieces of cake or cookies with whipped cream and fresh fruit to form a dessert parfait. Crumbled cookies also make an excellent ice cream or cream pie topping.

COUNTING CALORIES

BEVERAGES

apple juice, 6 oz.	90
coffee (black)	0
cola, 12 oz.	115
cranberry juice, 6 oz.	115
ginger ale, 12 oz.	115
grape juice, (prepared from frozen concentrate), 6 oz.	142
lemonade, (prepared from frozen concentrate), 6 oz.	85
milk, protein fortified, 1 c.	105
skim, 1 c.	90
whole, 1 c.	160
orange juice, 6 oz.	85
pineapple juice, unsweetened, 6 oz.	95
root beer, 12 oz.	150
tonic (quinine water) 12 oz.	132

BREADS

cornbread, 1 sm. square	130
dumplings, 1 med.	70
French toast, 1 slice	135
melba toast, 1 slice	25
muffins, blueberry, 1 muffin	110
bran, 1 muffin	106
corn, 1 muffin	125
English, 1 muffin	280
pancakes, 1 (4-in.)	60
pumpernickel, 1 slice	75
rye, 1 slice	60
waffle, 1	216
white, 1 slice	60 - 70
whole wheat, 1 slice	55 - 65

CEREALS

cornflakes, 1 c.	105
cream of wheat, 1 c.	120
oatmeal, 1 c.	148
rice flakes, 1 c.	105
shredded wheat, 1 biscuit	100
sugar krisps, 3/4 c.	110

CRACKERS

graham, 1 cracker	15 - 30
rye crisp, 1 cracker	35
saltine, 1 cracker	17 - 20
wheat thins, 1 cracker	9

DAIRY PRODUCTS

butter or margarine, 1 T.	100
cheese, American, 1 oz.	100
camembert, 1 oz.	85
cheddar, 1 oz.	115
cottage cheese, 1 oz.	30
mozzarella, 1 oz.	90
parmesan, 1 oz.	130
ricotta, 1 oz.	50
roquefort, 1 oz.	105
Swiss, 1 oz.	105
cream, light, 1 T.	30
heavy, 1 T.	55
sour, 1 T.	45
hot chocolate, with milk, 1 c.	277
milk chocolate, 1 oz.	145 - 155
yogurt	
made w/ whole milk, 1 c.	150 - 165
made w/ skimmed milk, 1 c.	125

EGGS

fried, 1 lg.	100
poached or boiled, 1 lg.	75 - 80
scrambled or in omelet, 1 lg.	110 - 130

FISH & SEAFOOD

bass, 4 oz.	105
salmon, broiled or baked, 3 oz.	155
sardines, canned in oil, 3 oz.	170
trout, fried, 3 1/2 oz.	220
tuna, in oil, 3 oz.	170
in water, 3 oz.	110

COUNTING CALORIES

FRUITS

apple, 1 med.	80 - 100
applesauce, sweetened, ½ c.	90 - 115
unsweetened, ½ c.	50
banana, 1 med.	85
blueberries, ½ c.	45
cantaloupe, ½ c.	24
cherries (pitted), raw, ½ c.	40
grapefruit, ½ med.	55
grapes, ½ c.	35 - 55
honeydew, ½ c.	55
mango, 1 med.	90
orange, 1 med.	65 - 75
peach, 1 med.	35
pear, 1 med.	60 - 100
pineapple, fresh, ½ c.	40
canned in syrup, ½ c.	95
plum, 1 med.	30
strawberries, fresh, ½ c.	30
frozen and sweetened, ½ c.	120 - 140
tangerine, 1 lg.	39
watermelon, ½ c.	42

MEAT & POULTRY

beef, ground (lean), 3 oz.	185
roast, 3 oz.	185
chicken, broiled, 3 oz.	115
lamb chop (lean), 3 oz.	175 - 200
steak, sirloin, 3 oz.	175
tenderloin, 3 oz.	174
top round, 3 oz.	162
turkey, dark meat, 3 oz.	175
white meat, 3 oz.	150
veal, cutlet, 3 oz.	156
roast, 3 oz.	76

NUTS

almonds, 2 T.	105
cashews, 2 T.	100
peanuts, 2 T.	105
peanut butter, 1 T.	95
pecans, 2 T.	95
pistachios, 2 T.	92
walnuts, 2 T.	80

PASTA

macaroni or spaghetti, cooked, ¾ c.	115

SALAD DRESSINGS

blue cheese, 1 T.	70
French, 1 T.	65
Italian, 1 T.	80
mayonnaise, 1 T.	100
olive oil, 1 T.	124
Russian, 1 T.	70
salad oil, 1 T.	120

SOUPS

bean, 1 c.	130 - 180
beef noodle, 1 c.	70
bouillon and consomme, 1 c.	30
chicken noodle, 1 c.	65
chicken with rice, 1 c.	50
minestrone, 1 c.	80 - 150
split pea, 1 c.	145 - 170
tomato with milk, 1 c.	170
vegetable, 1 c.	80 - 100

VEGETABLES

asparagus, 1 c.	35
broccoli, cooked, ½ c.	25
cabbage, cooked, ½ c.	15 - 20
carrots, cooked, ½ c.	25 - 30
cauliflower, ½ c.	10 - 15
corn (kernels), ½ c.	70
green beans, 1 c.	30
lettuce, shredded, ½ c.	5
mushrooms, canned, ½ c.	20
onions, cooked, ½ c.	30
peas, cooked, ½ c.	60
potato, baked, 1 med.	90
chips, 8-10	100
mashed, w/milk & butter, 1 c.	200 - 300
spinach, 1 c.	40
tomato, raw, 1 med.	25
cooked, ½ c.	30

COOKING TERMS

Au gratin: Topped with crumbs and/or cheese and browned in oven or under broiler.

Au jus: Served in its own juices.

Baste: To moisten foods during cooking with pan drippings or special sauce in order to add flavor and prevent drying.

Bisque: A thick cream soup.

Blanch: To immerse in rapidly boiling water and allow to cook slightly.

Cream: To soften a fat, especially butter, by beating it at room temperature. Butter and sugar are often creamed together, making a smooth, soft paste.

Crimp: To seal the edges of a two-crust pie either by pinching them at intervals with the fingers or by pressing them together with the tines of a fork.

Crudités: An assortment of raw vegetables (i.e. carrots, broccoli, celery, mushrooms) that is served as an hors d'oeuvre, often accompanied by a dip.

Degrease: To remove fat from the surface of stews, soups or stock. Usually cooled in the refrigerator so that fat hardens and is easily removed.

Dredge: To coat lightly with flour, cornmeal, etc.

Entrée: The main course.

Fold: To incorporate a delicate substance, such as whipped cream or beaten egg whites, into another substance without releasing air bubbles. A spatula is used to gently bring part of the mixture from the bottom of the bowl to the top. The process is repeated, while slowly rotating the bowl, until the ingredients are thoroughly blended.

Glaze: To cover with a glossy coating, such as a melted and somewhat diluted jelly for fruit desserts.

Julienne: To cut or slice vegetables, fruits or cheeses into match-shaped slivers.

Marinate: To allow food to stand in a liquid in order to tenderize or to add flavor.

Meuniére: Dredged with flour and sautéed in butter.

Mince: To chop food into very small pieces.

Parboil: To boil until partially cooked; to blanch. Usually final cooking in a seasoned sauce follows this procedure.

Pare: To remove the outermost skin of a fruit or vegetable.

Poach: To cook gently in hot liquid kept just below the boiling point.

Purée: To mash foods by hand by rubbing through a sieve or food mill, or by whirling in a blender or food processor until perfectly smooth.

Refresh: To run cold water over food that has been parboiled in order to stop the cooking process quickly.

Sauté: To cook and/or brown food in a small quantity of hot shortening.

Scald: To heat to just below the boiling point, when tiny bubbles appear at the edge of the saucepan.

Simmer: To cook in liquid just below the boiling point. The surface of the liquid should be barely moving, broken from time to time by slowly rising bubbles.

Steep: To let food stand in hot liquid in order to extract or to enhance flavor, like tea in hot water or poached fruit in syrup.

Toss: To combine ingredients with a repeated lifting motion.

Whip: To beat rapidly in order to incorporate air and produce expansion, as in heavy cream or egg whites.

PUBLISH
YOUR OWN
Cookbook

Churches, schools, organizations, families, and businesses can preserve their favorite recipes by publishing a custom cookbook. Cookbooks make a great **fundraiser** because they are easy to sell and highly profitable. Our low prices also make cookbooks a perfect affordable **keepsake**. We offer:

- Low prices, high quality, and prompt service.
- Many options and styles to suit your needs.
- 90 days to pay and a written No-Risk Guarantee.

Order our FREE Cookbook Kit for full details:

- Call us at **800-445-6621, ext. CB**.
- Visit our web site at **www.morriscookbooks.com**.
- Mail the **postage-paid reply card** below.

✂

ALL THE INGREDIENTS
FOR SUCCESS!™

Order our **FREE** Cookbook Kit. Please print neatly.

Name _____

Organization _____

Address_____

City _____ State _____ Zip _____

E-mail _____

Phone (_____) _____

Back Card 2-12

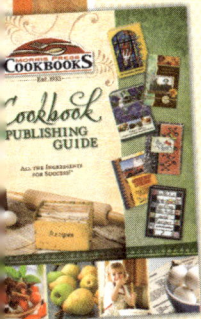

P.O. Box 2110
Kearney, NE 68848

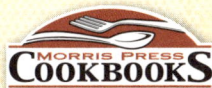

MORRIS PRESS
COOKBOOKS

PUBLISH
YOUR OWN
Cookbook

Whether your goal is to raise funds or create a cherished keepsake, Morris Press Cookbooks has all the right ingredients to make a great custom cookbook. Raise **$500 – $50,000** or more while preserving favorite recipes.

Three ways to order our **FREE** Cookbook Kit:
- Call us at **800-445-6621, ext. CB**.
- Visit our web site at **www.morriscookbooks.com**.
- Complete and mail the **reply card** below.

ALL THE INGREDIENTS FOR SUCCESS![TM]

Use your smart phone QR app to learn more.